RECORDED VERSIONS GUITAR

ACCURATE TAB EDITION

ERIC CLAPTON   I STILL DO

T0065912

Music transcriptions by Pete Billmann and Jeff Jacobson

ISBN 978-1-4950-7183-6

HAL•LEONARD®

7777 W. BLUEMOUND RD. P.O. BOX 13819 MILWAUKEE, WI 53213

Visit Hal Leonard Online at
www.halleonard.com

Alabama Woman Blues

Words and Music by Leroy Carr

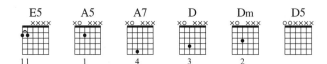

Gtr. 1: Open A tuning:
(low to high) E-A-E-A-C#-E

Gtr. 2: Drop D tuning:
(low to high) D-A-D-G-B-E

Key of A

Intro
Slow ♩ = 63

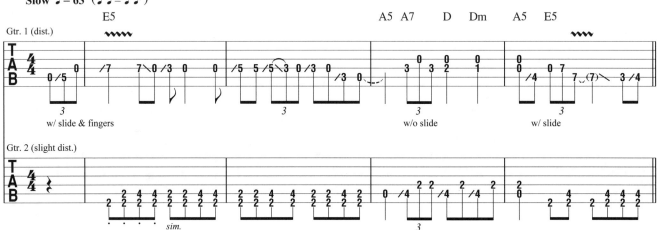

Verse

1. D'ya ev-er go down   Mo-bile and K. C. line?

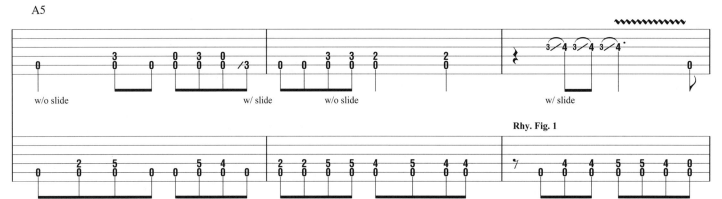

You ev-er go down   on the Mo-bile and K. C. line?

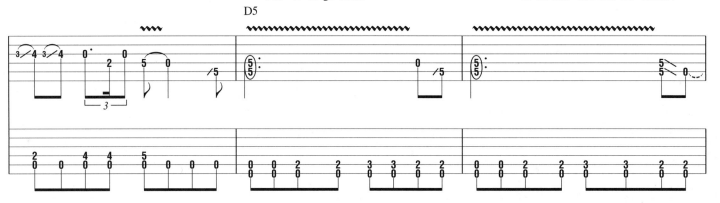

Just wan-na ask you,

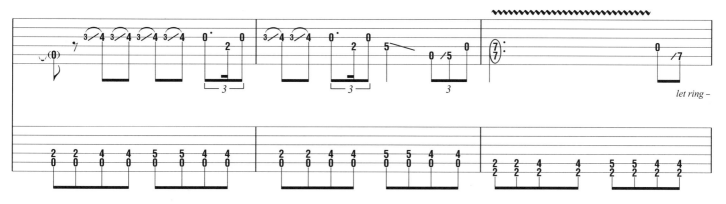

d'you ev - er see that gal of mine?

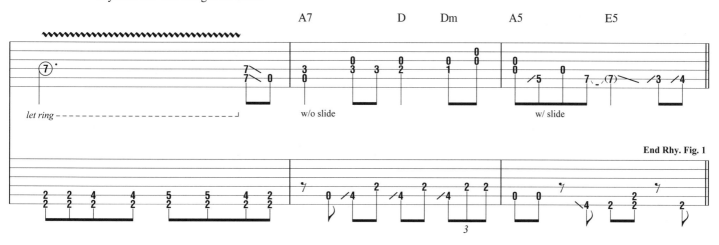

Verse

2. I rode the Cen - tral and I hus-tled the L and N.

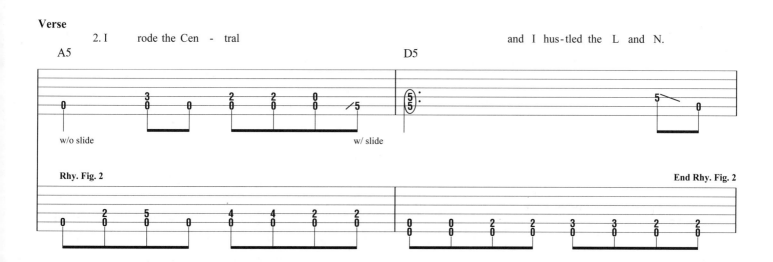

Gtr. 2: w/ Rhy. Fig. 1

I rode the Cen-tral

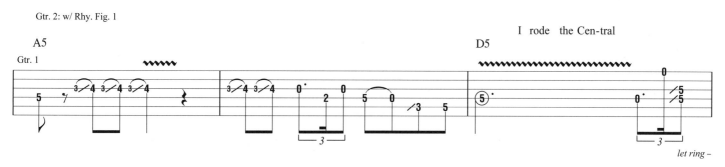

and I hus - tled the L and N.

A5

let ring

Al-a-ba-ma wom-en,   they live like sec-tion men.

E5   A7   D   Dm   A5   E5

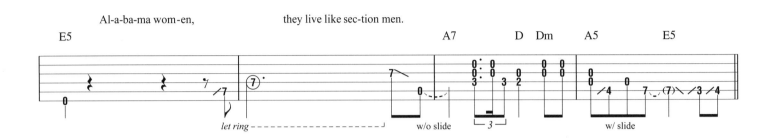

let ring   w/o slide   w/ slide

Verse

Gtr. 2: w/ Rhy. Fig. 2   Gtr. 2: w/ Rhy. Fig. 1

Don't cry, babe.   Your pa-pa will be home some day.

A5   D5   A5

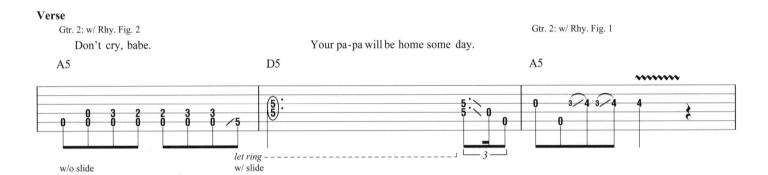

w/o slide
w/ slide   let ring

Don't cry, ba - by.   Your pa-pa will be home some day.

D5

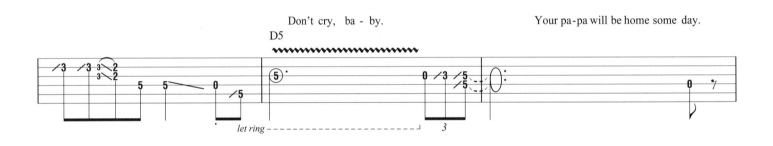

let ring

I   went a-way, ba-by,

A5   E5

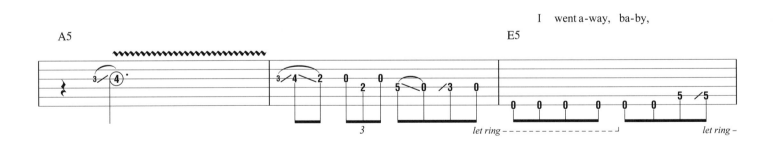

let ring   let ring -

but I did not go to stay.

A7   D   Dm   A5   E5

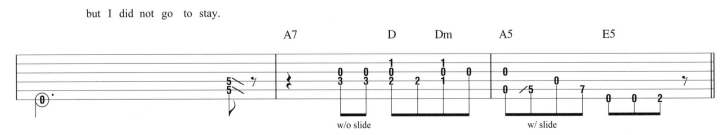

w/o slide   w/ slide

Guitar Solo

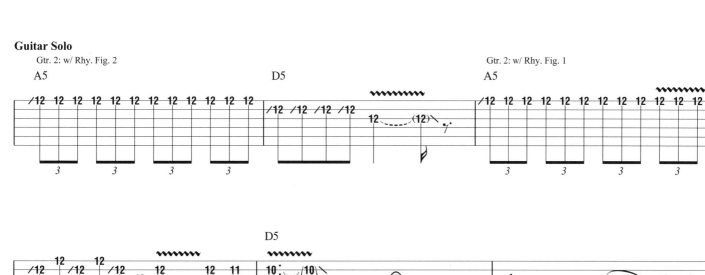

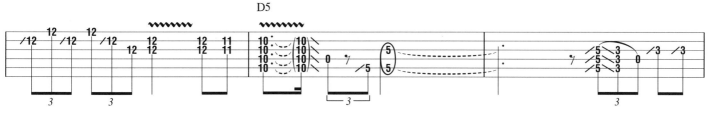

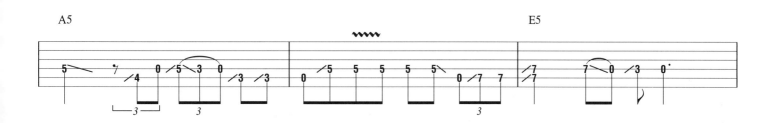

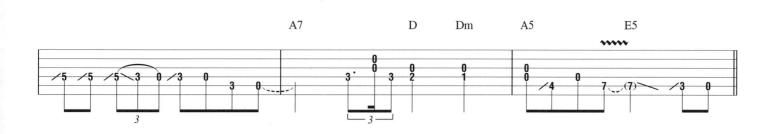

Verse

Gtr. 2: w/ Rhy. Fig. 2

4. Don't the clouds look lone-some 'cross the deep blue sea?

Gtr. 2: w/ Rhy. Fig. 1

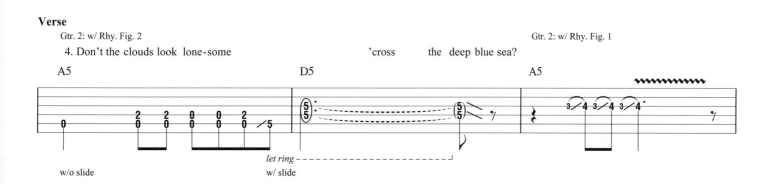

w/o slide

w/ slide

let ring

Don't the clouds look lone-some 'cross the deep blue sea?

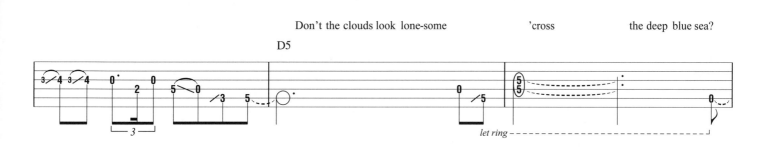

let ring

Don't my gal look good

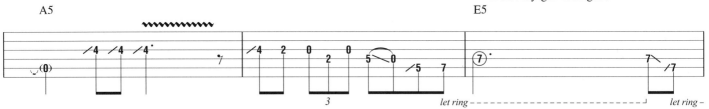

when she com-in' af - ter me?

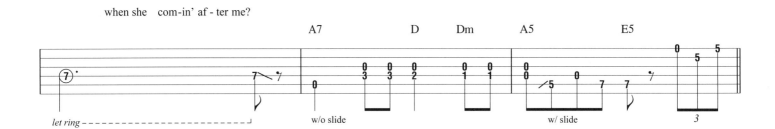

Outro-Guitar Solo

Gtr. 2: w/ Rhy. Fig. 2

Gtr. 2: w/ Rhy. Fig. 1 (1st 7 meas.)

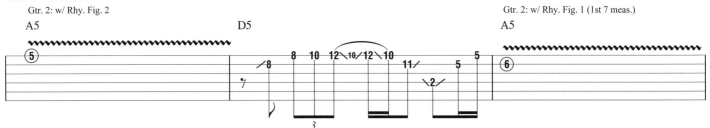

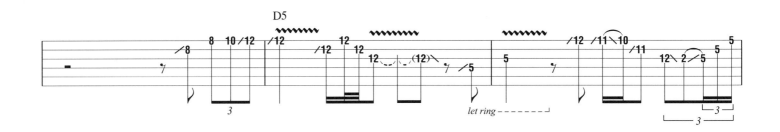

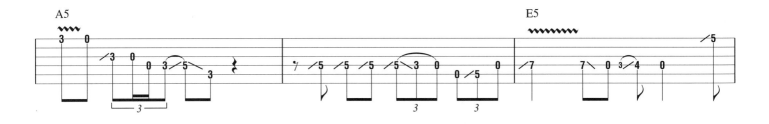

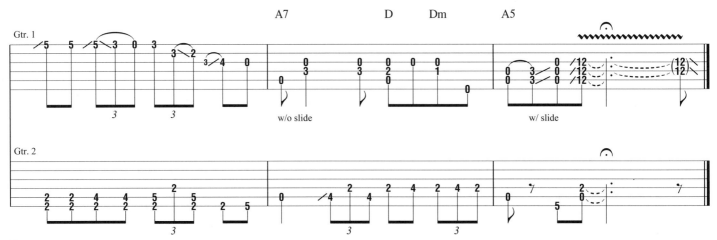

Can't Let You Do It

Words and Music by J.J. Cale

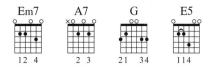

Gtr. 4: Open E tuning:
(low to high) E-B-E-G#-B-E

Key of Em
Intro
Moderately ♩ = 100

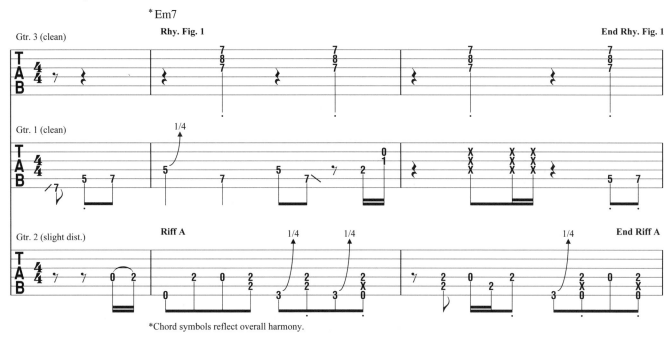

*Chord symbols reflect overall harmony.

Gtr. 2: w/ Riff A (3 times)
Gtr. 3: w/ Rhy. Fig. 1 (3 times)

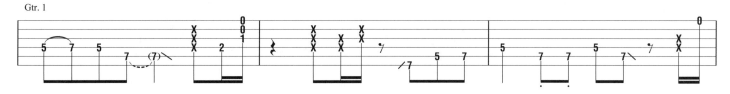

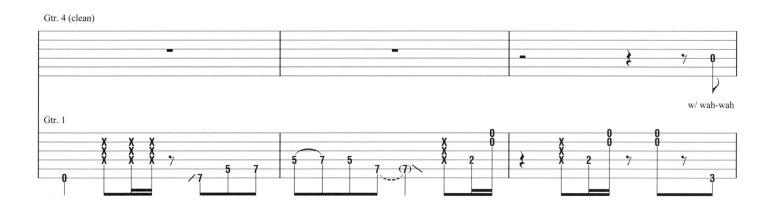

w/ wah-wah

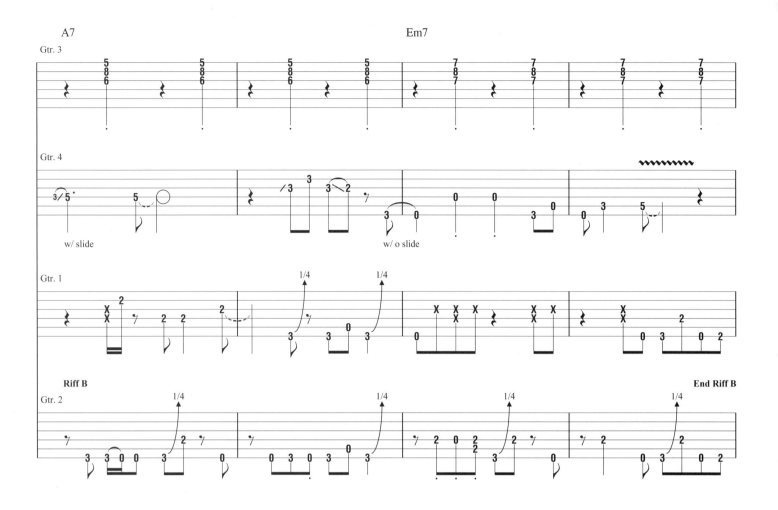

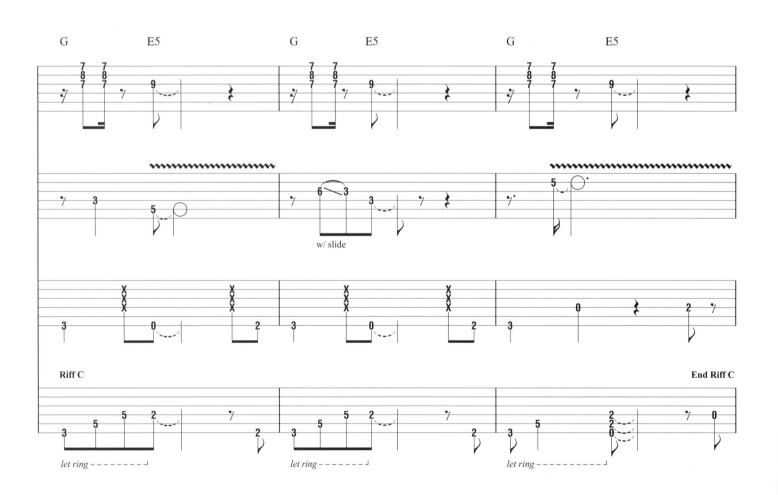

Gtr. 2: w/ Riff A (2 times)
Gtr. 3: w/ Rhy. Fig. 1 (2 times)
Gtr/. 4 tacet

1. Well, you

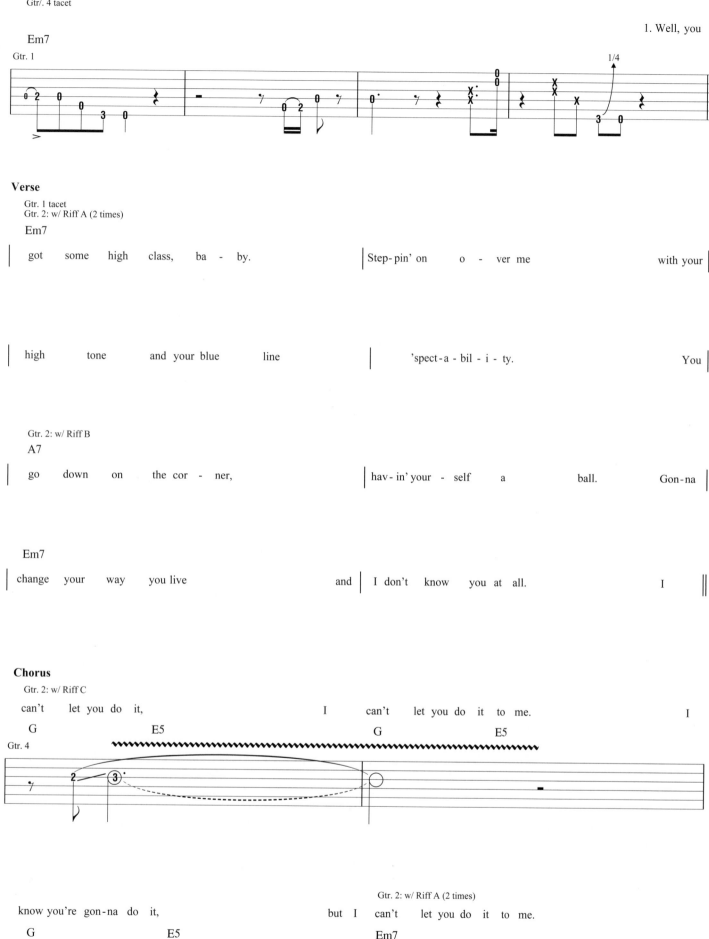

Verse

Gtr. 1 tacet
Gtr. 2: w/ Riff A (2 times)

Em7

got some high class, ba - by.   Step-pin' on   o - ver me   with your

high   tone   and your blue   line   'spect-a - bil - i - ty.   You

Gtr. 2: w/ Riff B

A7

go   down   on   the cor - ner,   hav-in' your - self   a   ball.   Gon-na

Em7

change   your   way   you live   and   I don't   know   you at all.   I

Chorus

Gtr. 2: w/ Riff C

can't   let you do it,   I   can't   let you do it to me.   I
G   E5   G   E5

Gtr. 2: w/ Riff A (2 times)

know you're gon-na do it,   but I   can't   let you do it to me.
G   E5   Em7

9

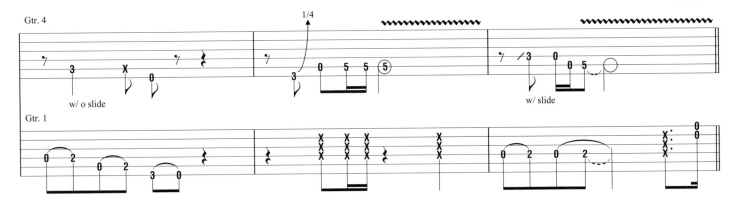

Verse

Gtrs. 1 & 4 tacet
Gtr. 2: w/ Riff A (2 times)

Em7

sun don't shine no more and the | blue sky don't ap - pear. The |

rain - fall don't fall no more. I | real - ly don't think you care. You |

Gtr. 2: w/ Riff B

got so wrapped up, ba - by, in ev - 'ry - thing you do. Been

A7

put - tin' on the dog, you know. And I mean you. I

Em7

Chorus

Gtr. 2: w/ Riff C

can't let you do it, I | can't let you do it to me. | I know you're gon - na do it, but I |

G5   E5   G5   E5   G5   E5

Guitar Solo

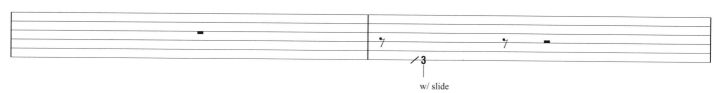

Gtr. 2: w/ Riff A (4 1/2 times)

can't   let you do it to me.

Em7

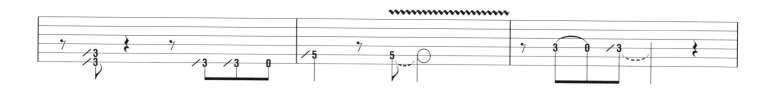

w/ slide

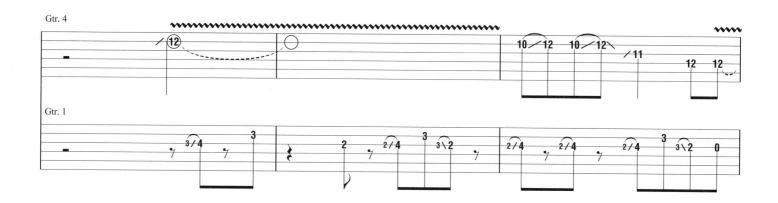

Gtr. 4

Gtr. 1

Gtr. 2: w/ Riff B

A7

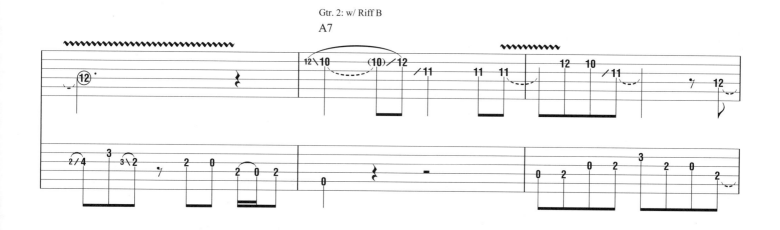

Em7   Gtr. 2: w/ Riff C

G   E5

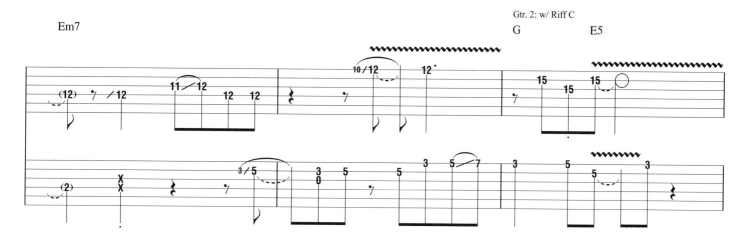

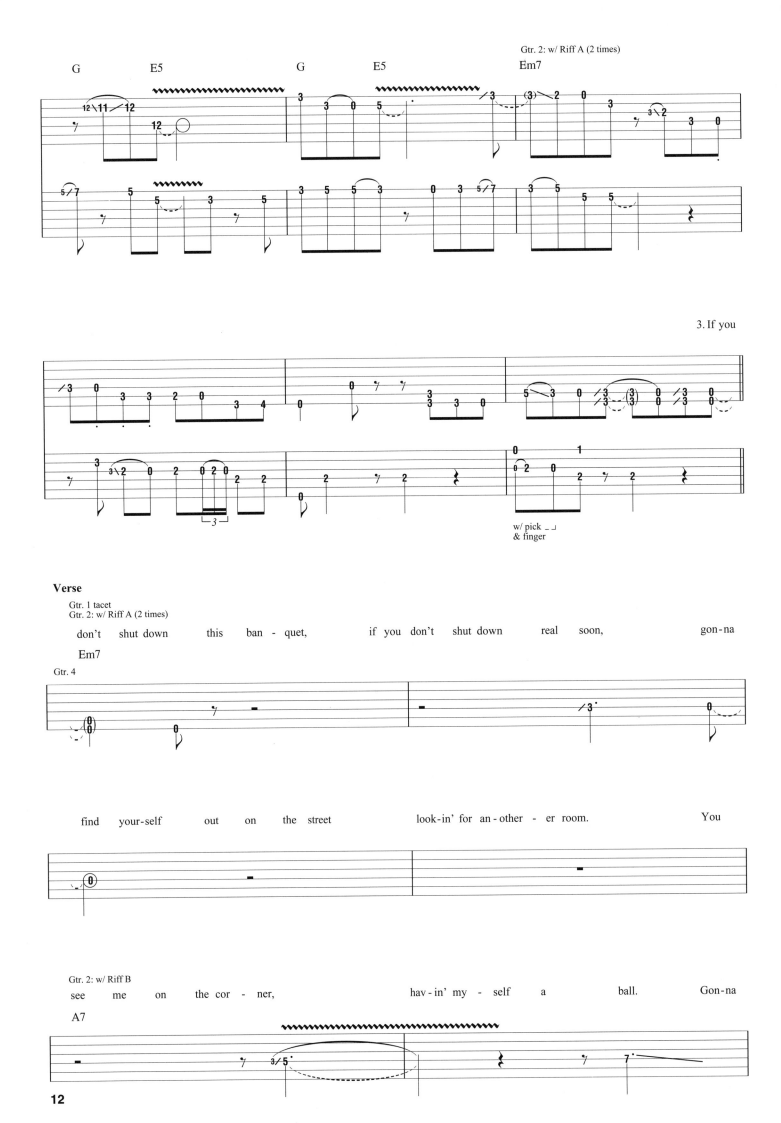

Gtr. 2: w/ Riff A (2 times)

G   E5   G   E5   Em7

3. If you

Verse

Gtr. 1 tacet
Gtr. 2: w/ Riff A (2 times)

don't   shut   down   this   ban - quet,   if   you   don't   shut   down   real   soon,   gon-na

Em7

Gtr. 4

find   your-self   out   on   the   street   look-in'   for   an - oth - er   room.   You

Gtr. 2: w/ Riff B

see   me   on   the   cor - ner,   hav - in'   my - self   a   ball.   Gon-na

A7

change my way of liv - in'   and you won't know me at all.   I

Em7

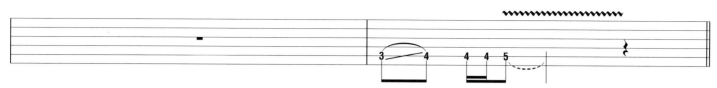

Chorus

Gtr. 2: w/ Riff C

can't let you do it,   I can't let you do it to me.   I

G   E5   G5   E5

G5   E5   Gtr. 2: w/ Riff A (2 times)

know you're gon-na do it,   but I   can't let you do it to me.

Em7

Gtr. 4

Gtr. 1

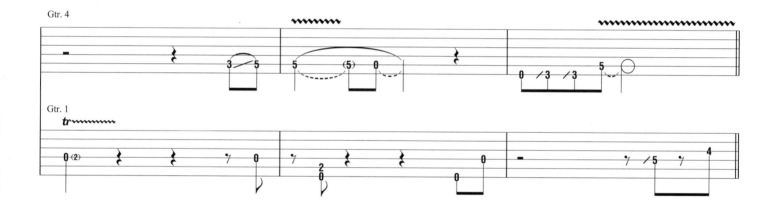

Outro-Guitar Solo

Gtr. 2: w/ Riff A (till fade)

Em7

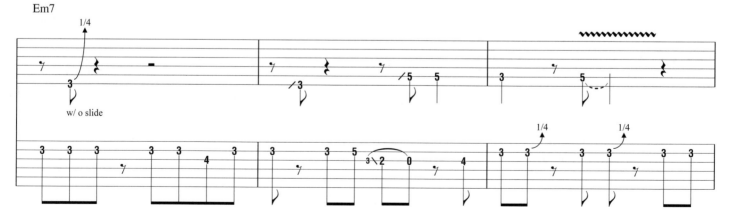

13

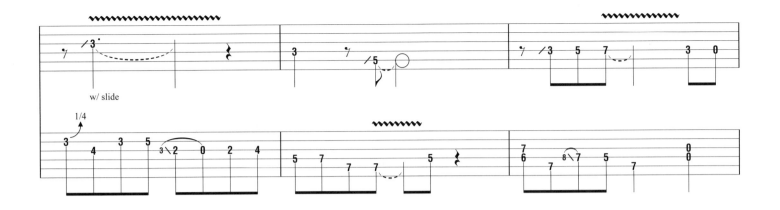

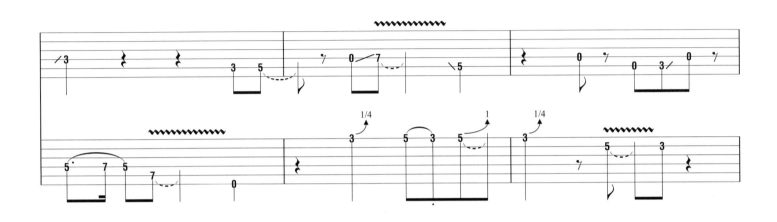

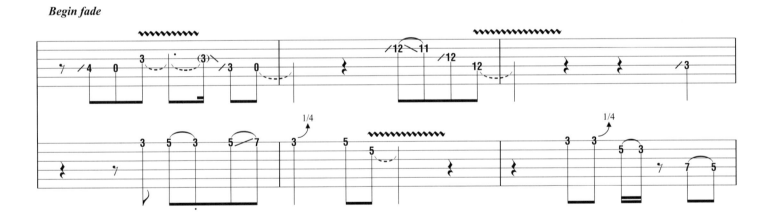

Begin fade

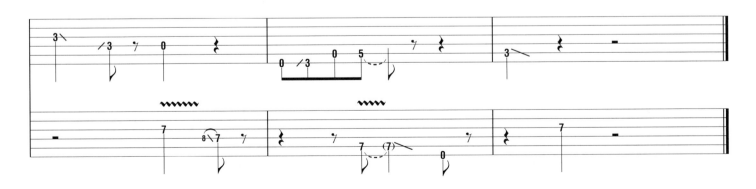

Fade out

I Will Be There

Words and Music by John O'Kane and Paul Brady

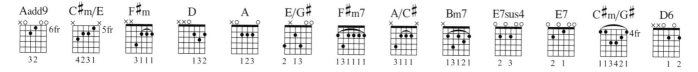

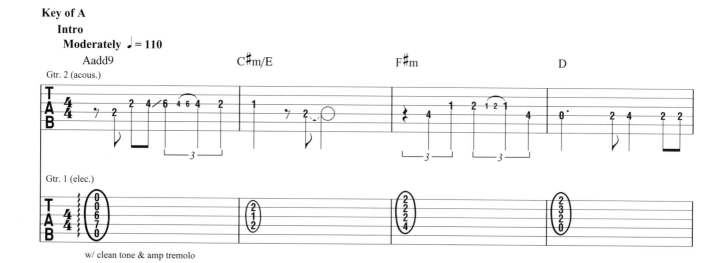

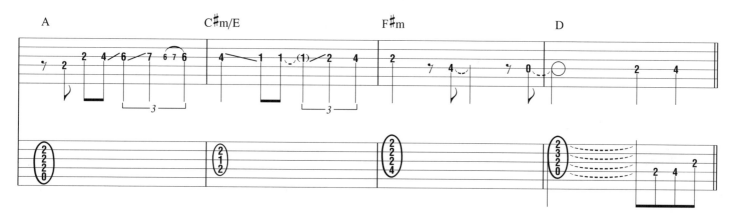

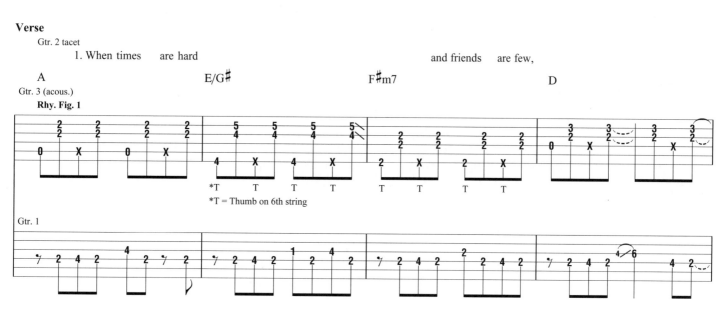

you need   some-one   to help   you through...

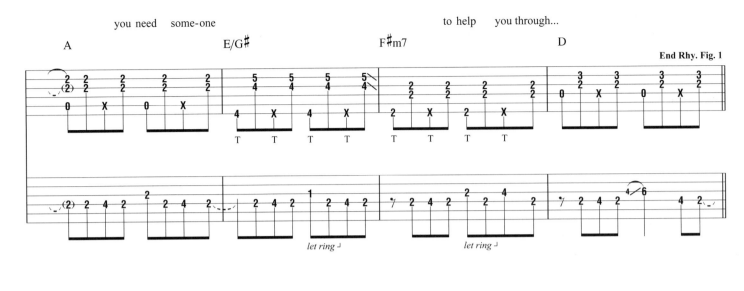

Pre-Chorus
Just   call   my name,   and I will come run - ning   to your side.

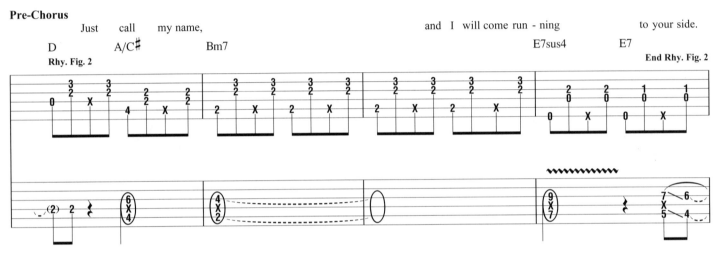

Don't   be   a-fraid,   don't be   a-fraid.   I   will   be there.

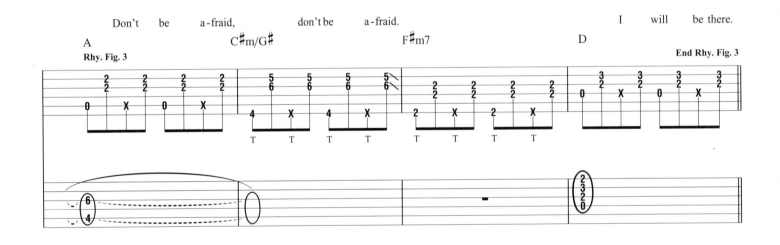

Chorus
Gtr. 3: w/ Rhy. Fig. 3

I will   be there.   I   will   be there.

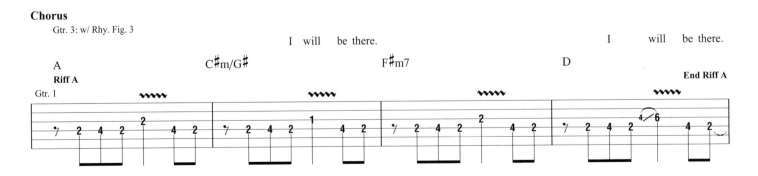

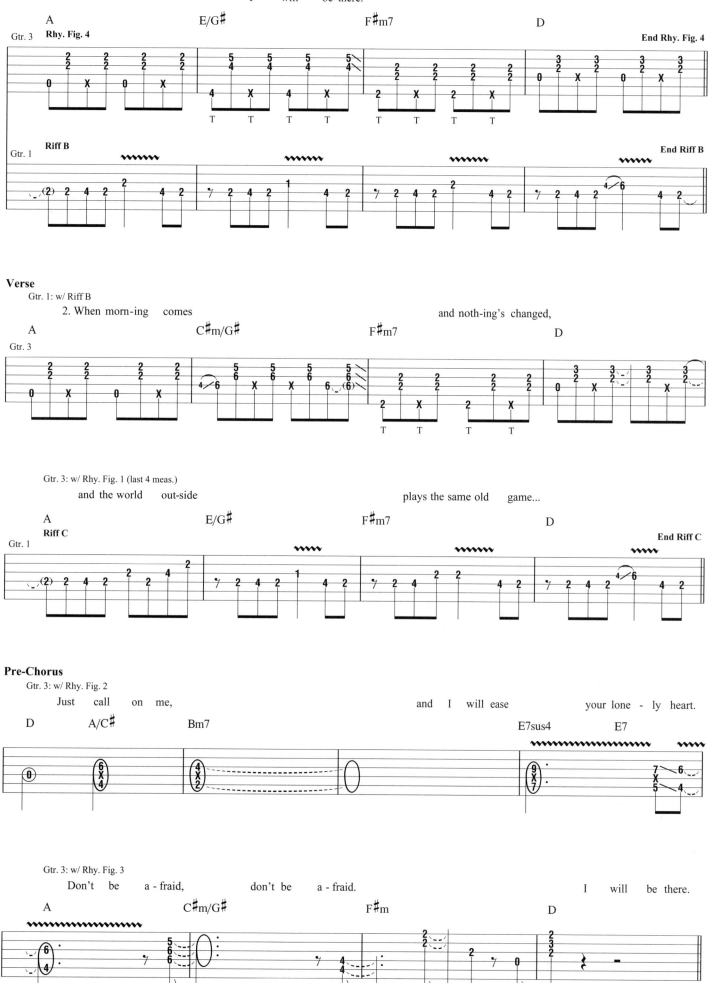

𝄉 Chorus

Gtr. 1: w/ Riff A
Gtr. 3: w/ Rhy. Fig. 4 (4 times)

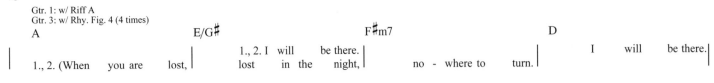

| A | E/G♯ | F♯m7 | D |

1., 2. (When you are lost,   1., 2. I will be there.   lost in the night,   no - where to turn.   I will be there.

1st time, Gtr. 1: w/ Riff C
2nd time, Gtr. 1: w/ Riff B (3 times)

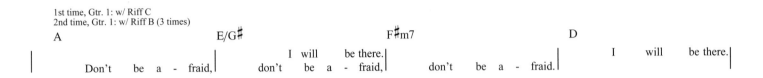

| A | E/G♯ | F♯m7 | D |

Don't be a - fraid,   don't be a - fraid,   I will be there.   don't be a - fraid.   I will be there.

When ev -'ry - one   that you be - lieve   I will be there.   still lets you down.   I will be there.

| A | C♯m/E | F♯m7 | D6 |

Gtr. 1

Rhy. Fig. 5   **End Rhy. Fig. 5**

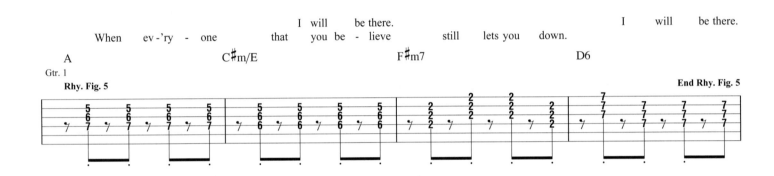

1st time, Gtr. 1: w/ Rhy. Fig. 5

| A | E/G♯ | F♯m7 | D6 |

Don't be a - fraid,   I will be there   don't be a - fraid,   don't be a - fraid.)

Interlude

1st time, Gtr. 1: w/ Rhy. Fig. 5 (2 times)
2nd time, Gtr. 1: w/ Riff B (2 times)
Gtr. 3: w/ Rhy. Fig. 1

| A | E/G♯ | F♯m7 | D6 |

Gtr. 2

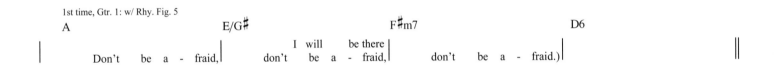

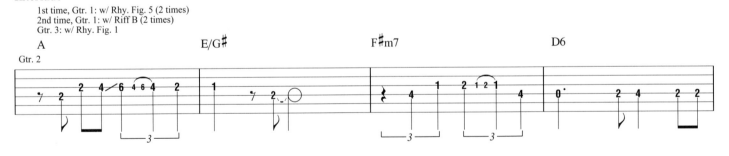

To Coda ⊕

| A | E/G♯ | F♯m7 | D6 |

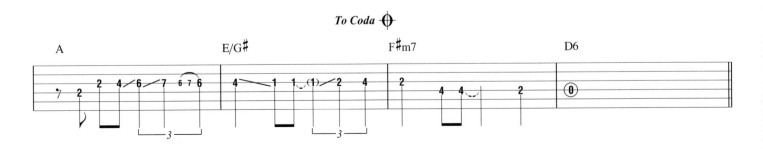

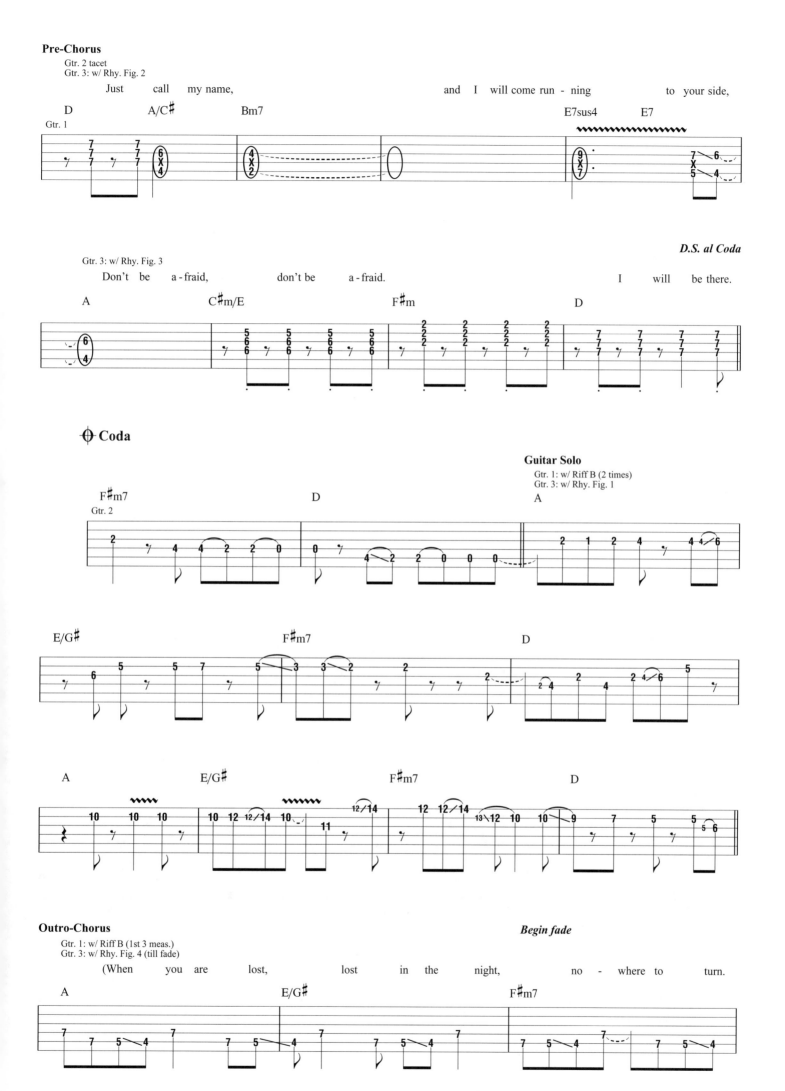

Don't be a - fraid, don't be a - fraid,

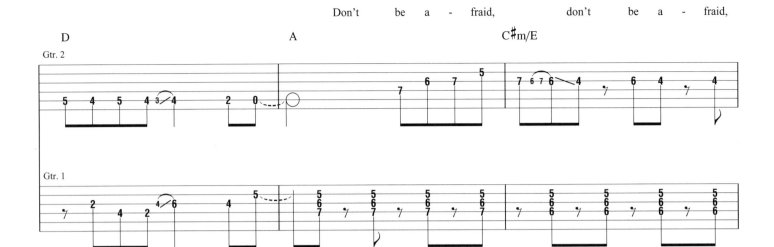

don't be a - fraid. When ev - 'ry - one

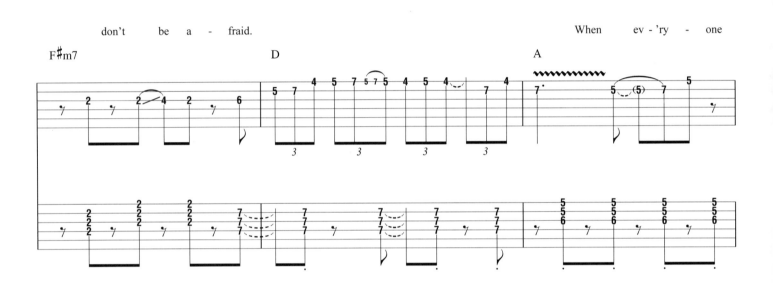

Fade out

that you be - lieve still lets you down.)

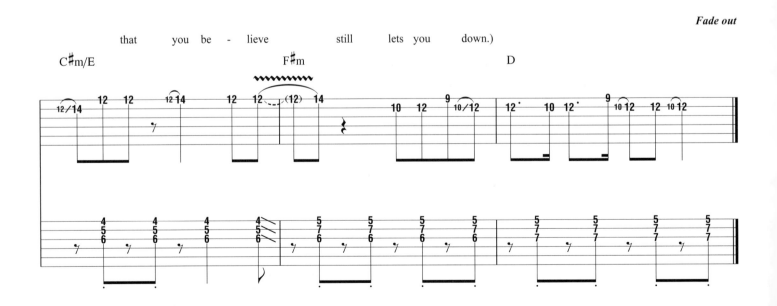

Spiral

Words and Music by Eric Clapton, Andy Fairweather-Low and Simon Climie

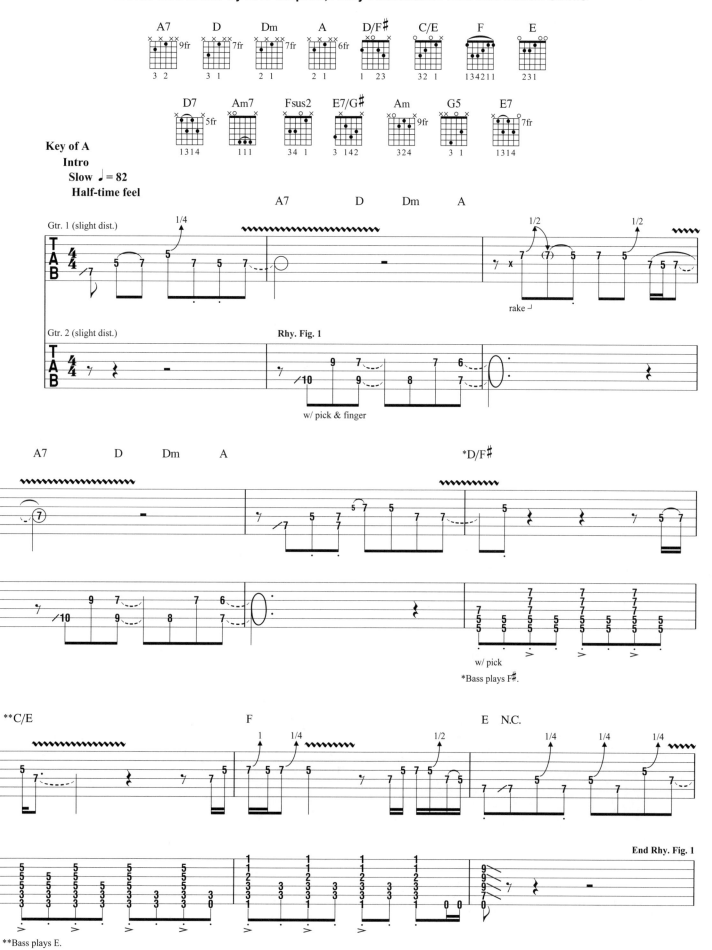

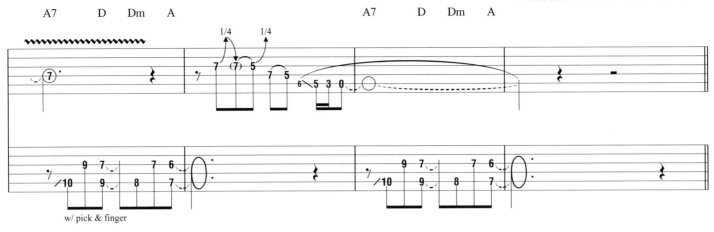

Verse

Gtr. 2: w/ Rhy. Fig. 1

to have this mu-sic in me.

I just keep play-in' these blues,

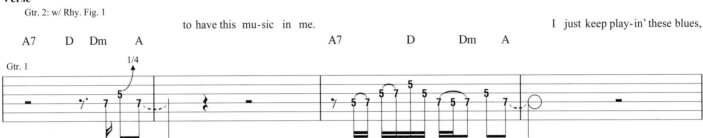

hop-in' that I don't lose.

2. I just keep play-in' my song,

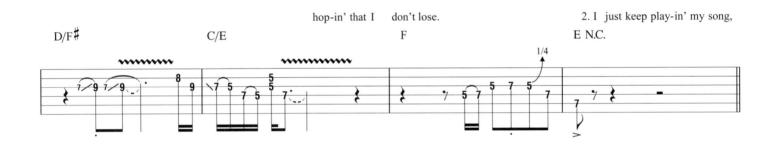

Verse

Gtr. 2: w/ Rhy. Fig. 1

hop-in' that I get a-long.

You don't know how much it means

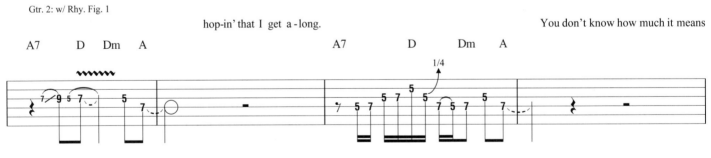

to have this mu-sic in me.

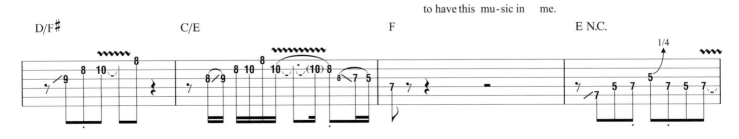

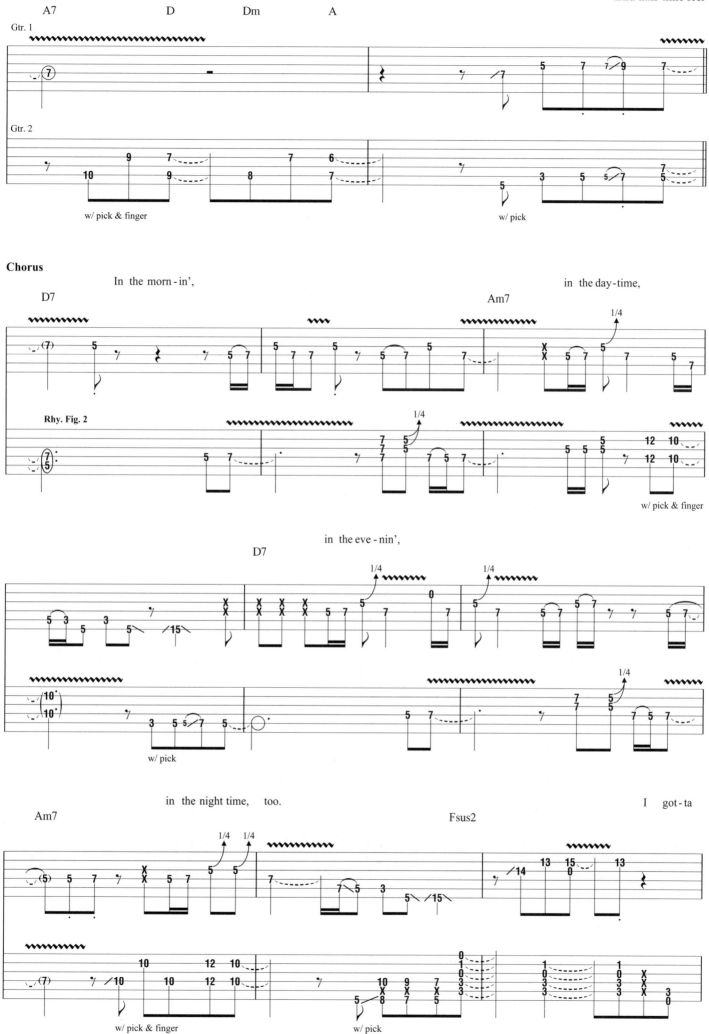

have it,   I got-ta have this.

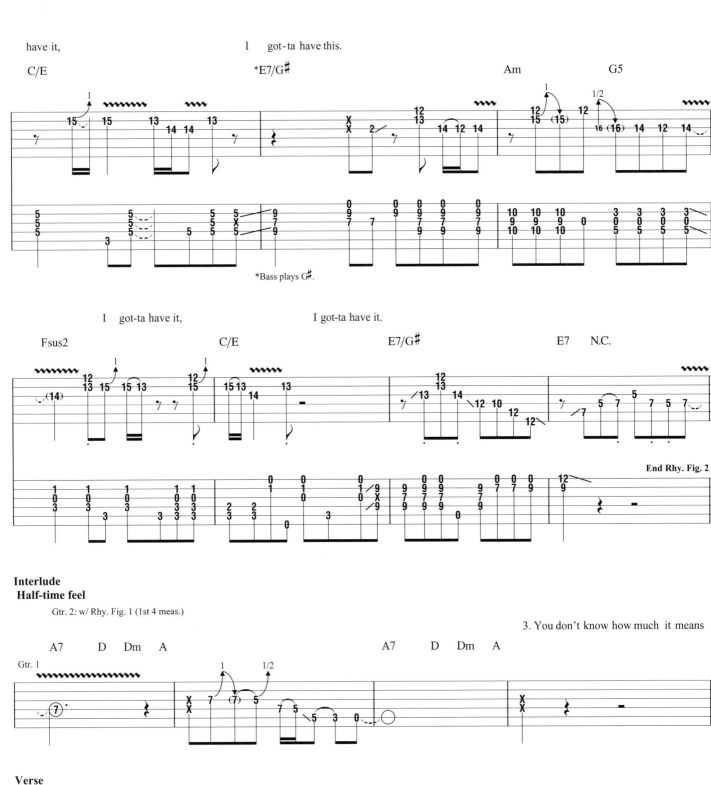

*Bass plays G♯.

I got-ta have it,   I got-ta have it.

End Rhy. Fig. 2

Interlude
Half-time feel

Gtr. 2: w/ Rhy. Fig. 1 (1st 4 meas.)

3. You don't know how much it means

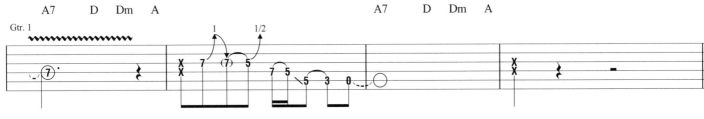

Verse
Gtr. 2: w/ Rhy. Fig. 1

to have this mu-sic in me.   I just keep play-in' my song,

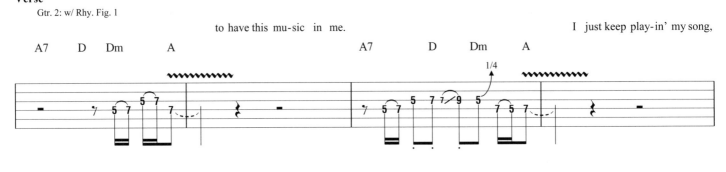

hop-in' that I get a-long.

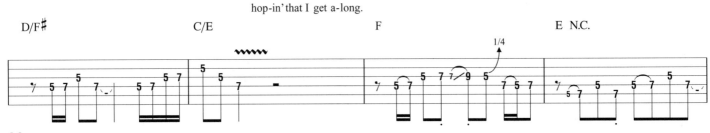

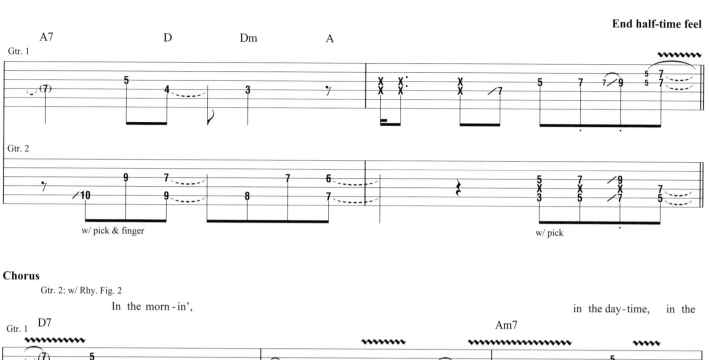

Chorus

Gtr. 2: w/ Rhy. Fig. 2

In the morn-in', in the day-time, in the

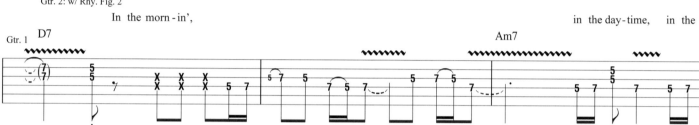

night, in the night time, too. In the morn-in', in the day-time, in the eve-nin',

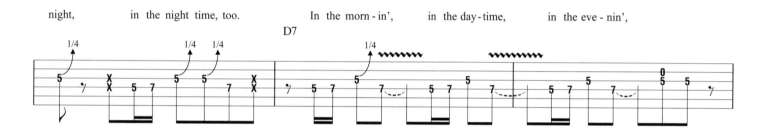

in the mid-night hour. I got-ta have it,

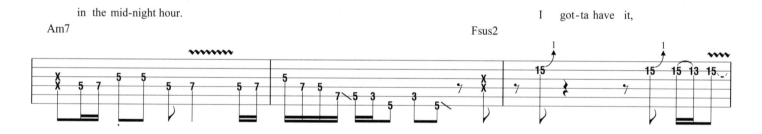

I got-ta have it, I got-ta have this blues.

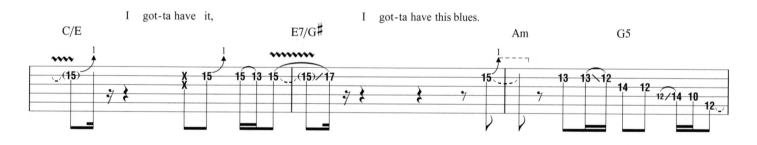

I got-ta have it, I got-ta have...

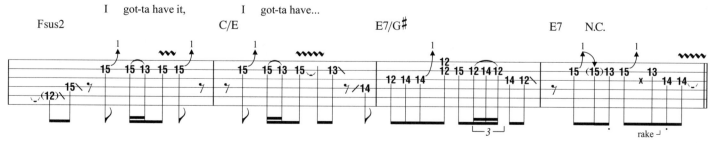

Outro-Guitar Solo
Half-time feel

Gtr. 2: w/ Rhy. Fig. 1 (1st 4 meas., 5 times)

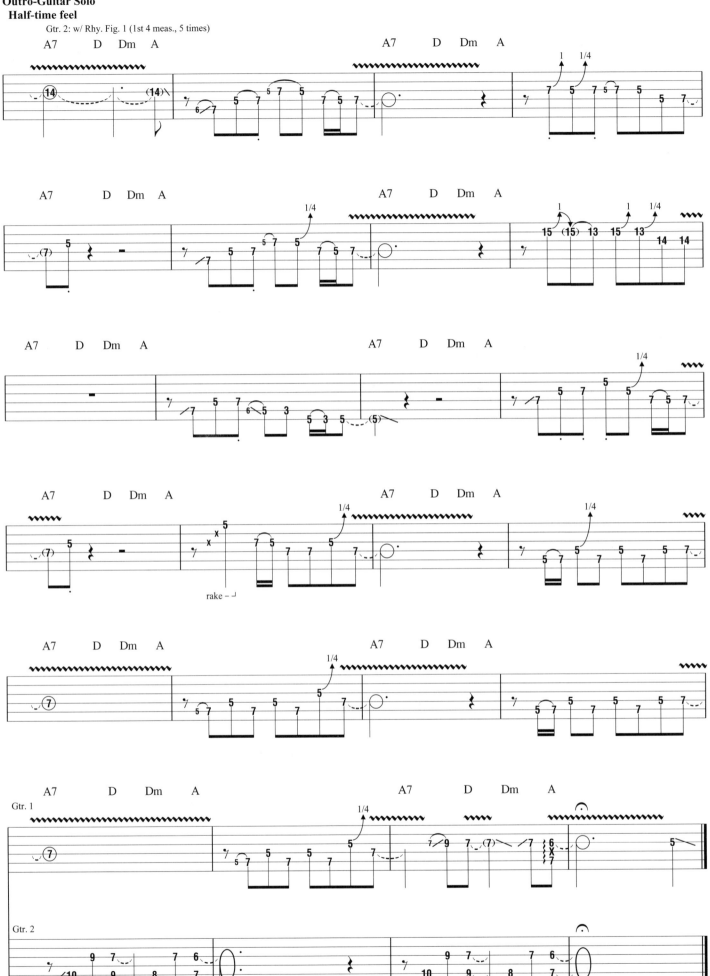

Catch the Blues

Words and Music by Eric Clapton

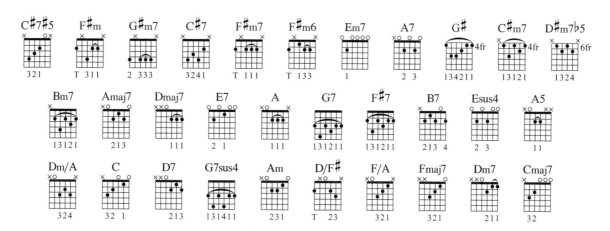

Key of F#m

Intro

Moderately ♩ = 108

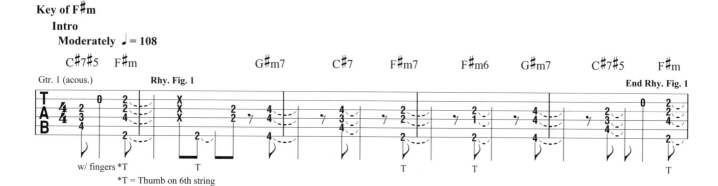

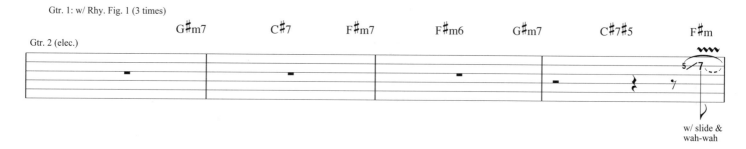

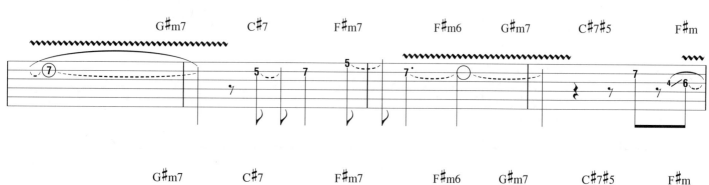

Verse

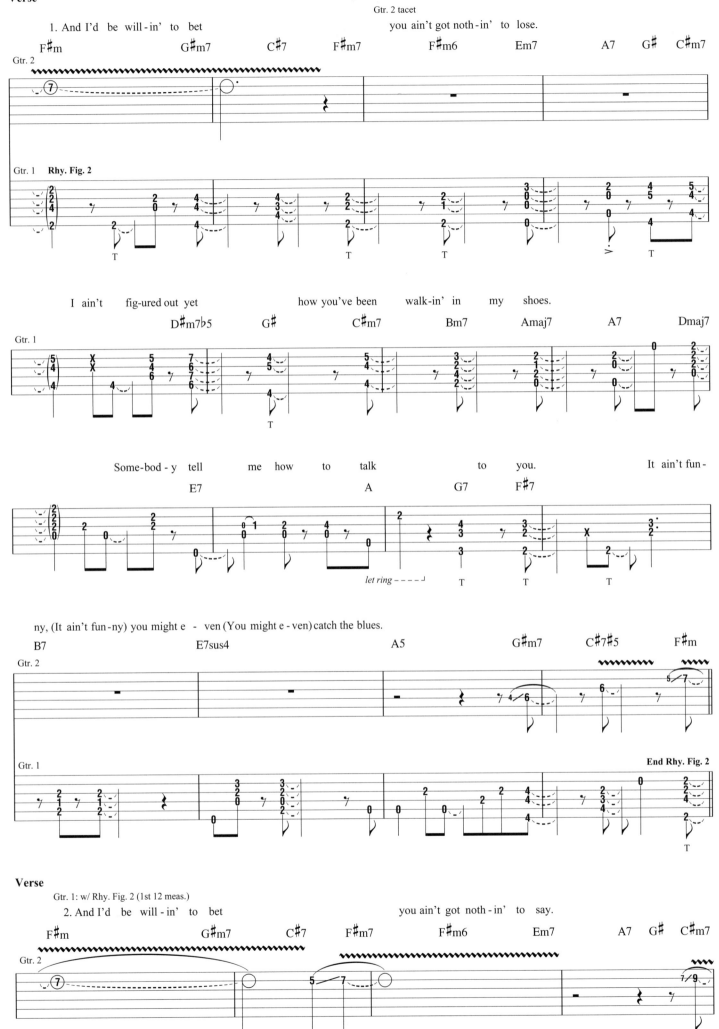

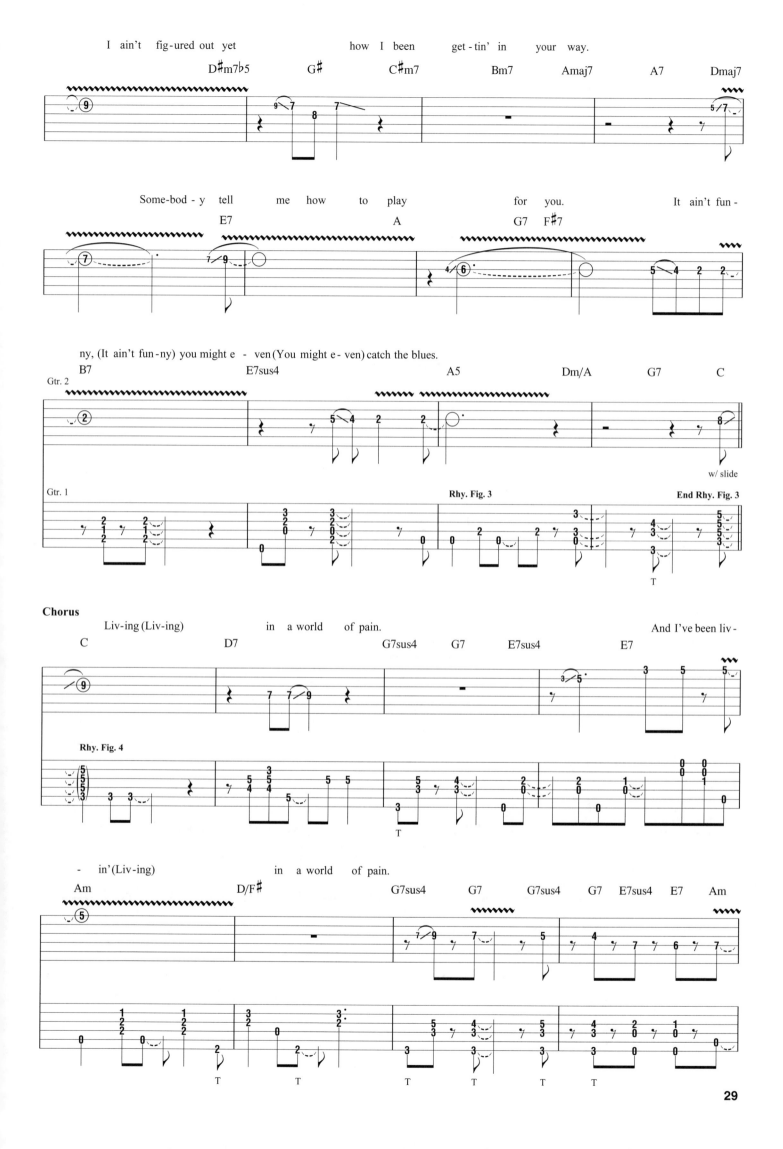

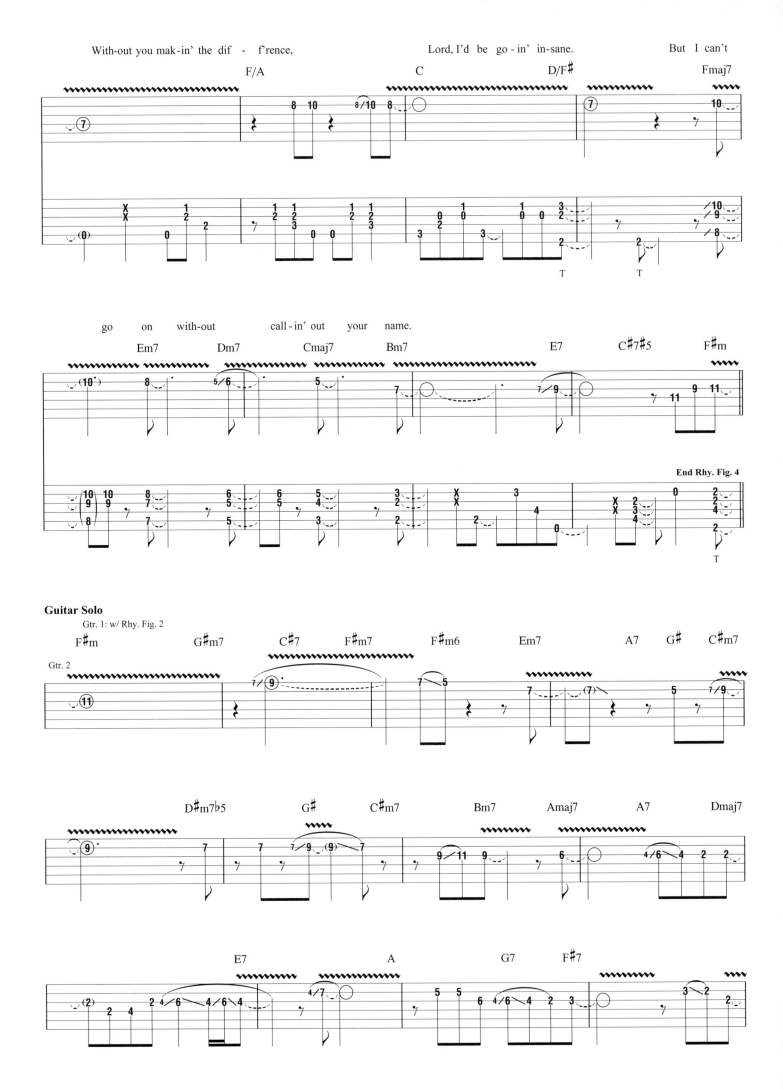

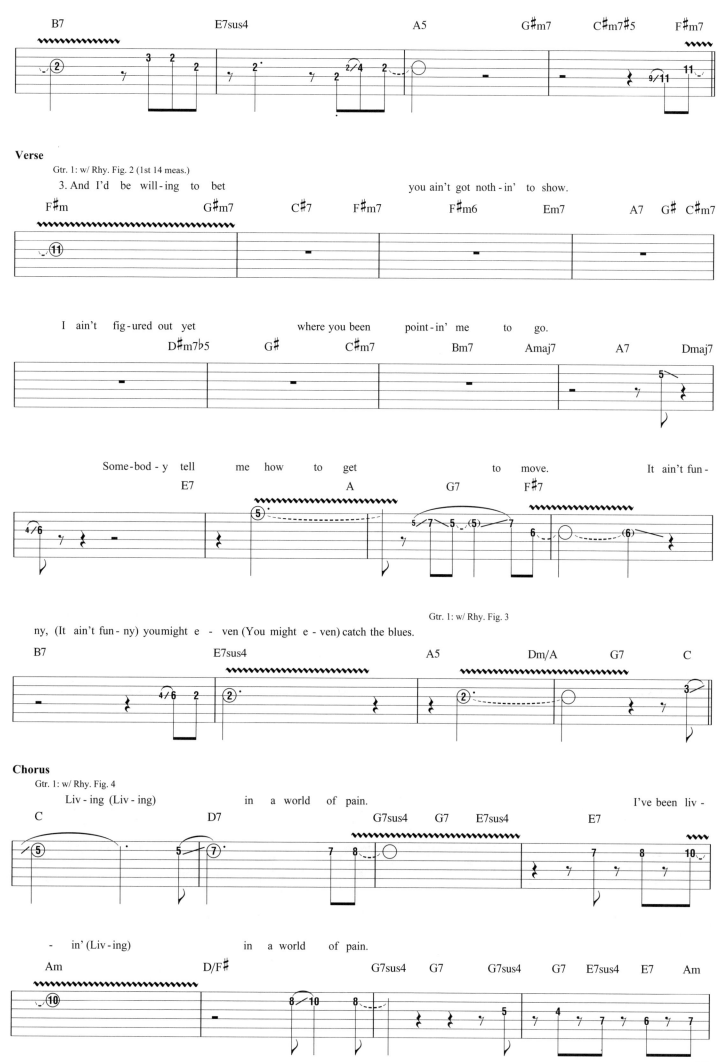

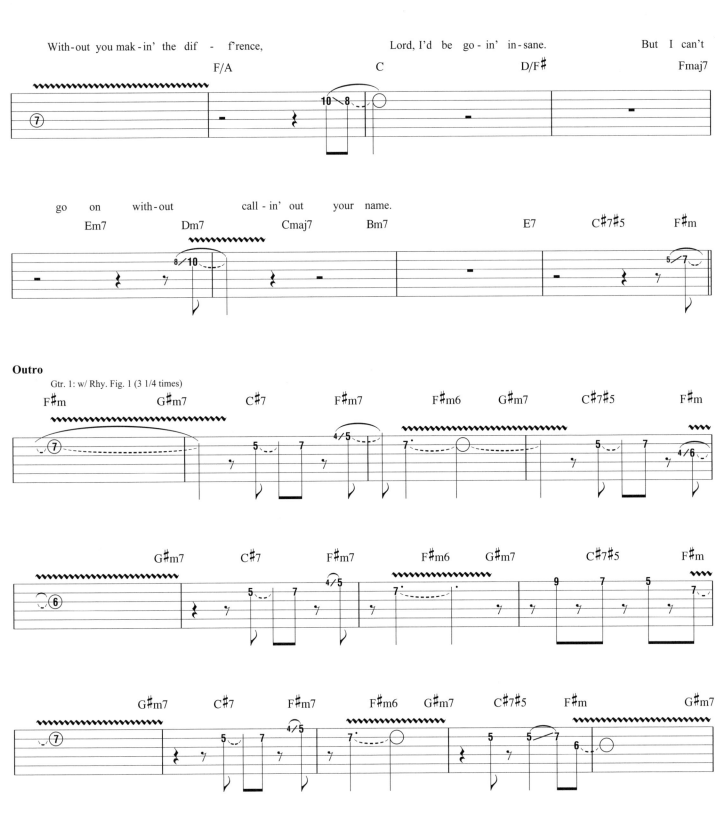

Outro

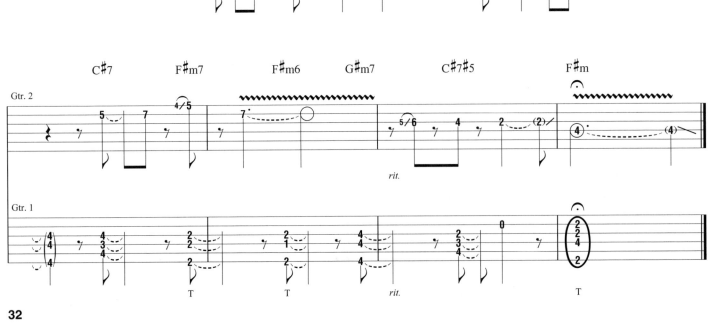

Cypress Grove

Words and Music by Nehemiah "Skip" James

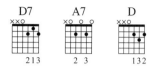

Gtr. 1: Open D tuning:
(low to high) D-A-D-F#-A-D

Key of D
Intro
Moderately slow ♩ = 96

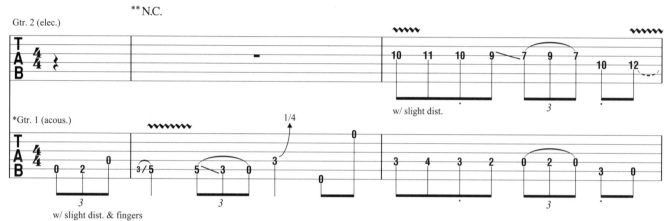

w/ slight dist.

*Gtr. 1 (acous.)

w/ slight dist. & fingers
*w/ slide on pinky (not used till indicated).
**Chord symbols reflect basic harmony.

Half-time feel

D7

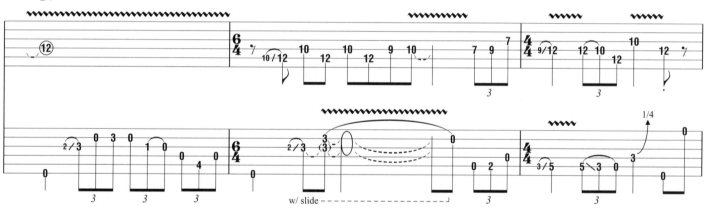

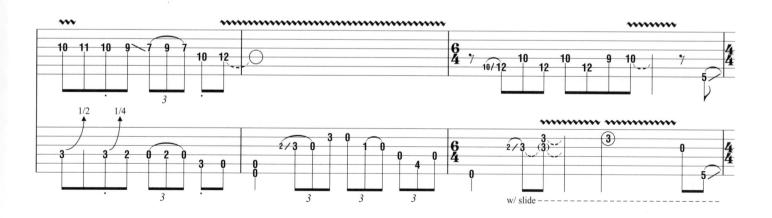

A7

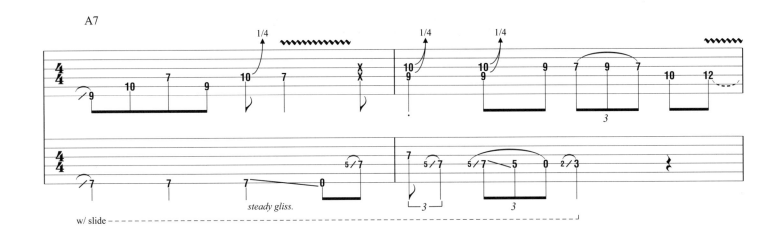

1. I   would

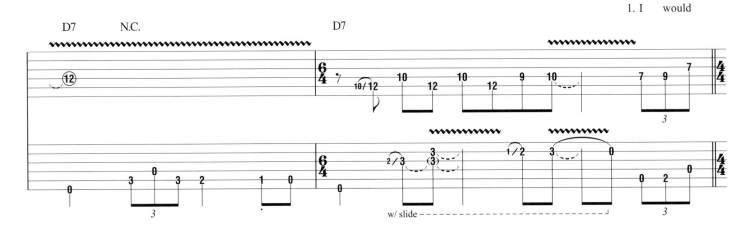

Verse

rath - er   be   bur - ied   in   some   cy - press   grove...
knee - bone's   get - tin'   shak - y,   hon - ey,   and   your   blood   runs   cold...
rath - er   be   bur - ied   six   feet   in   the   clay...

D7

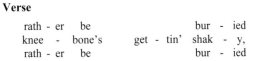

I   would
And when your
Oh, and I'd

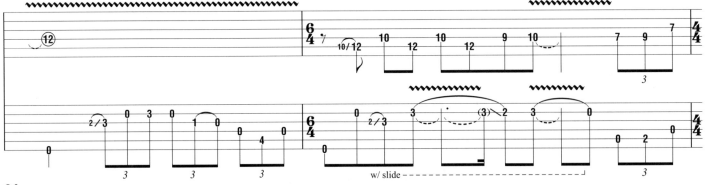

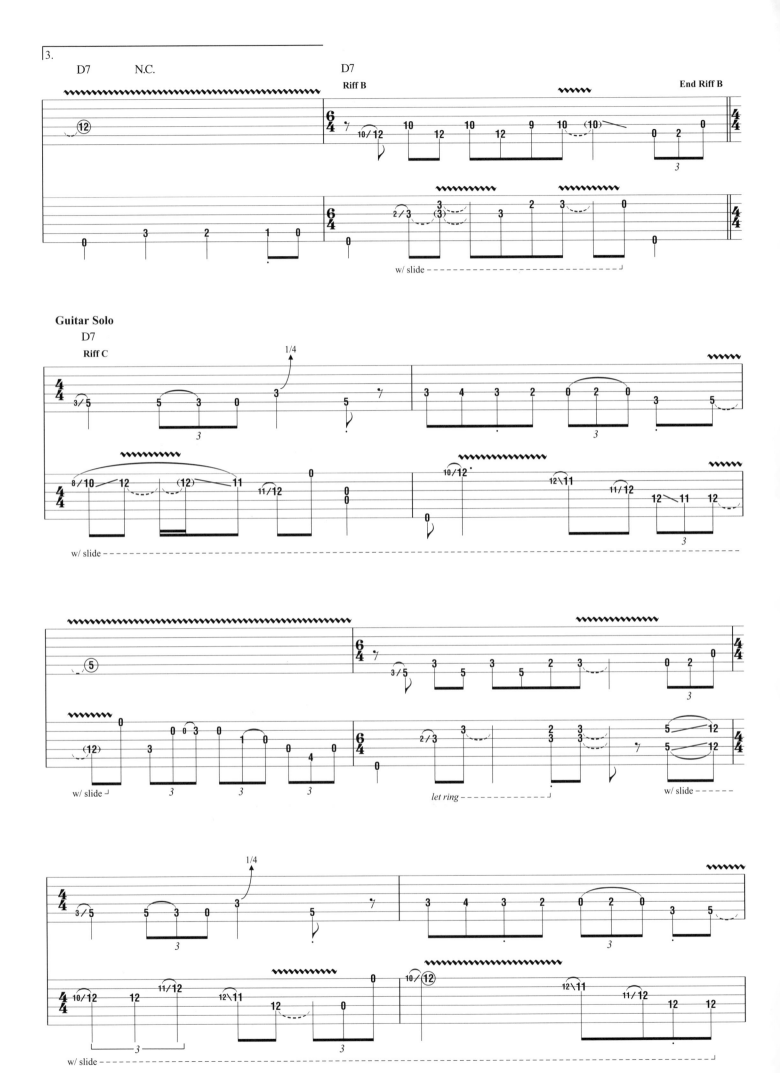

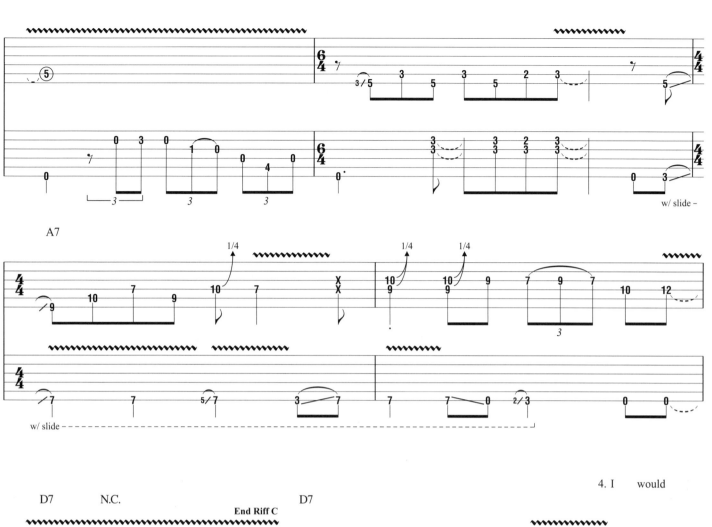

A7

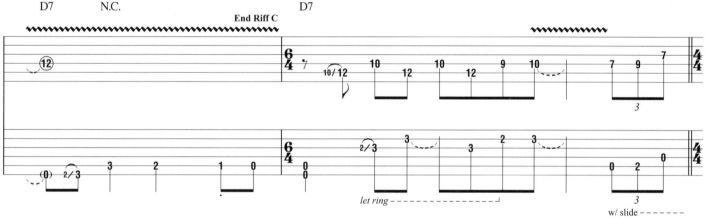

4. I would

D7　　　N.C.　　　　　　　　　　　　D7

End Riff C

Verse

Gtr. 2: w/ Riff A

drink mud-dy wa-ter, sleep in a hol-low log...

D7

Gtr. 1

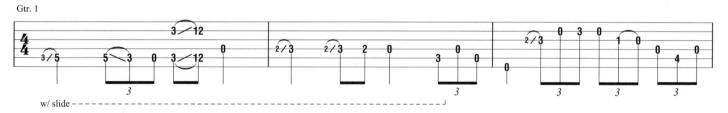

I would drink mud-dy wa-ter, sleep in a hol-low log

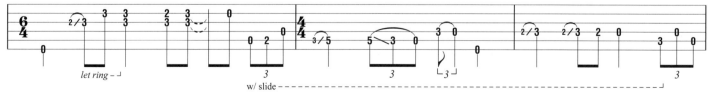

than to   stay   'round   here

A7

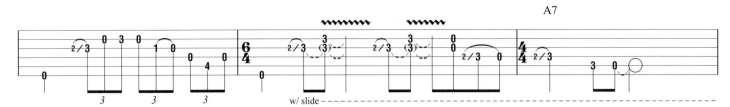

treat - ed   like   a dog.   5. I ain't gon - na

D7 N.C.   D7

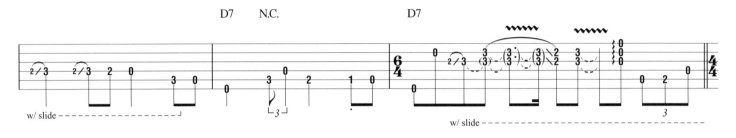

Verse

Gtr. 2: w/ Riff A (1st 11 meas.)

sing   this   song,   ain't   gon - na sing   no more.

D7

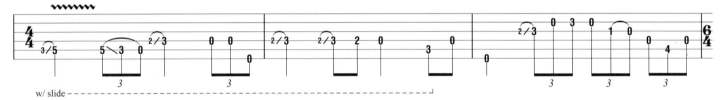

I ain't gon - na   sing   this   song,   ain't   gon - na sing   no more.

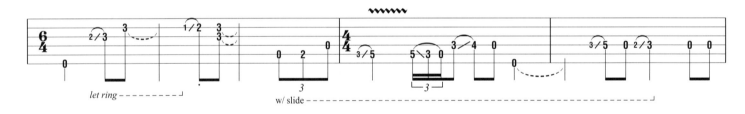

My   time is get - tin' pre - cious,

A7

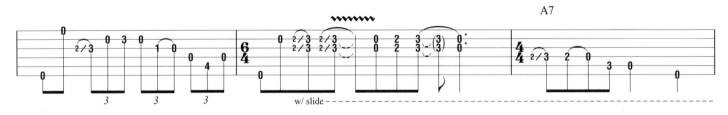

Gtr. 2: w/ Riff B

hon - ey, and I got   to go.

D7 N.C.   D7

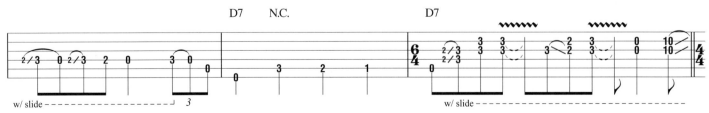

Outro-Guitar Solo

Gtr. 2: w/ Riff C

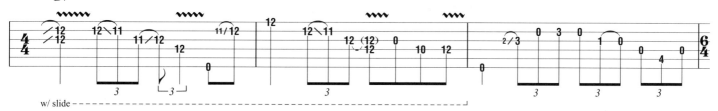

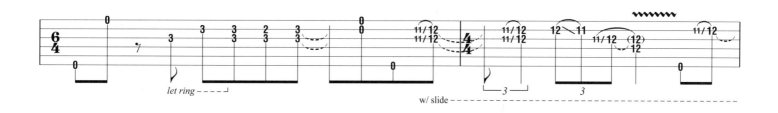

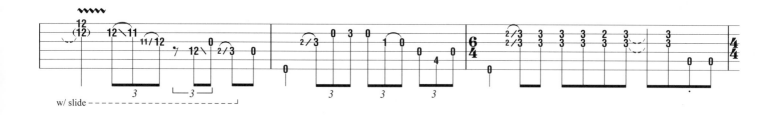

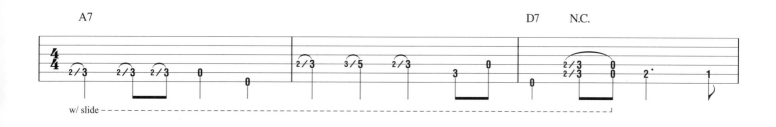

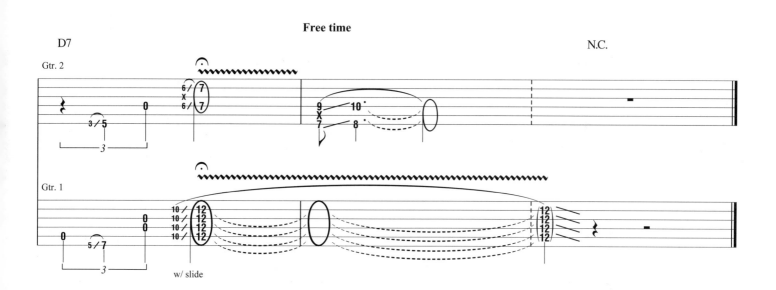

Little Man You've Had a Busy Day

Words by Maurice Sigler and Al Hoffman
Music by Mabel Wayne

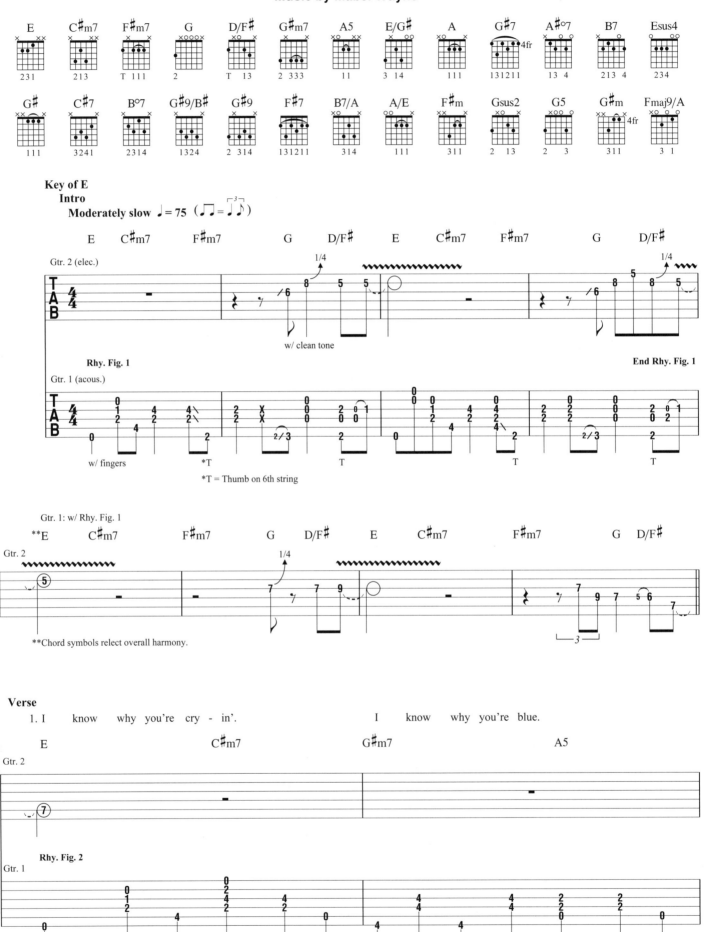

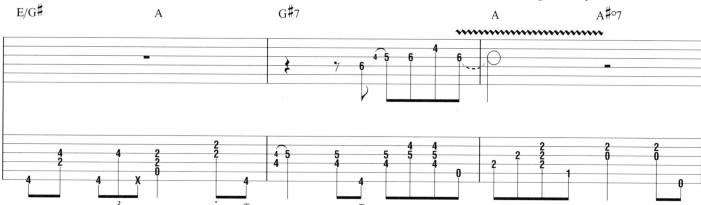

Some-one took your kid-dy car a-way.   Time to go to sleep, now.

Lit-tle man, you've had a bus-y day.

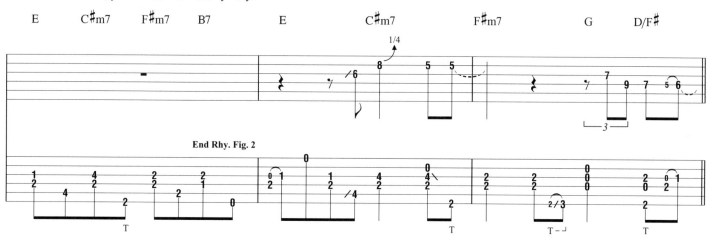

End Rhy. Fig. 2

Verse

Gtr. 1: w/ Rhy. Fig. 2

2. Some-one took your mar-bles,   tell you what I'll do.   Dad-'ll buy some new ones right a-

way.   Time to go to sleep, now.   Lit-tle man, you've had a bus-y day.

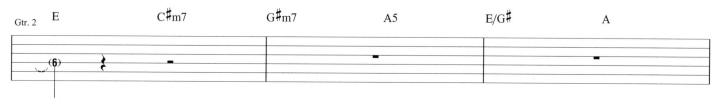

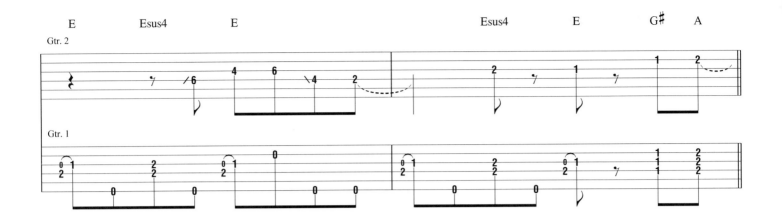

Bridge

Gtr. 2 tacet

Put a - way your sol - diers, the bat - tle has been won. The

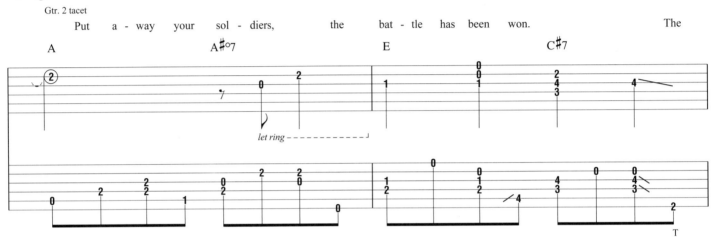

en - e - my is out of sight. Come a - long now, sol - dier, and

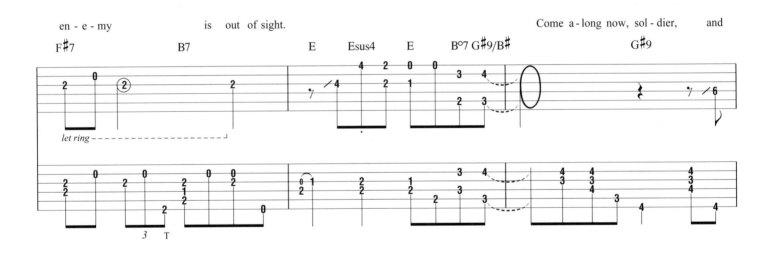

put a - way your gun. The war is o - ver for to - night.

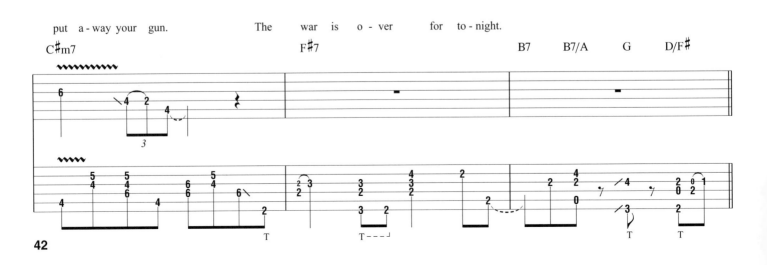

Verse

Gtr. 1: w/ Rhy. Fig. 2

| E | C#m7 | G#m7 | A5 | E/G# | A |

3. Time to   stop your schem-in',   time your day was through.   Lis-ten to the juke-box   soft-ly

play.   It's time to go to sleep, now.   Lit-tle man, you've had a bus-y day.

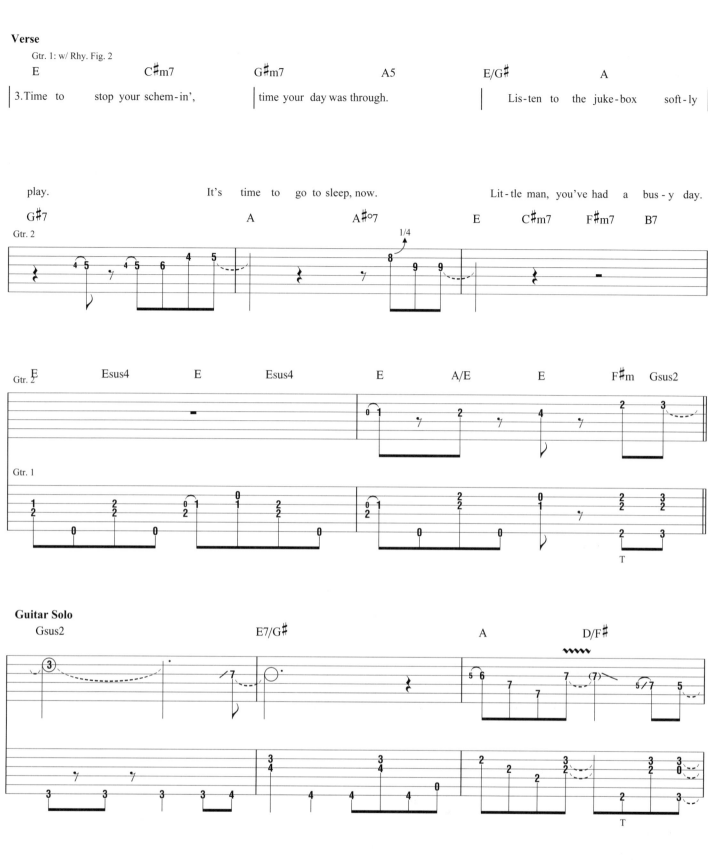

Guitar Solo

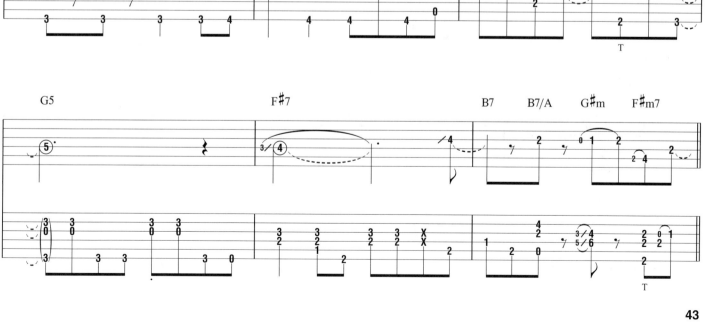

Verse

Gtr. 1: w/ Rhy. Fig. 2

4. Time to   stop your schem - in',   time this day was through.   Lis-ten to   the juke-box   soft-ly

E   C#m7   G#m7   A5   E/G#   A

Gtr. 2

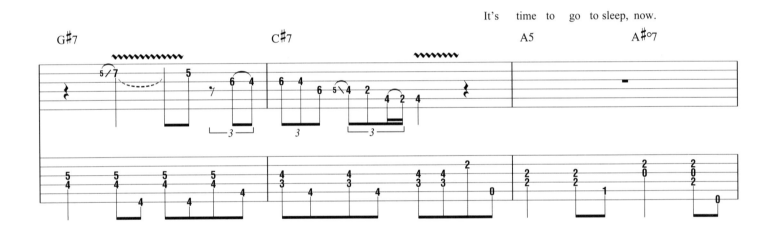

play.   It's   time to   go to sleep, now.   Lit - tle man, you've had   a   bus - y day.

G#7   A   A#°7   E   C#m7   F#m7   B7

1/4

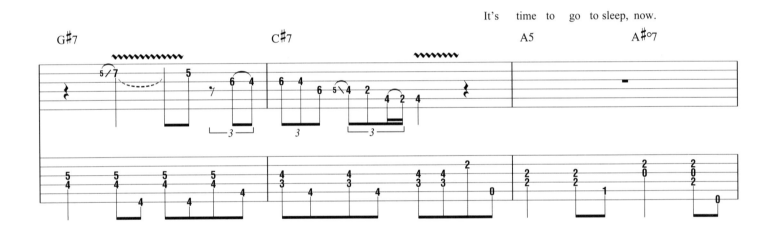

It's   time to   go to sleep, now.

G#7   C#7   A5   A#°7

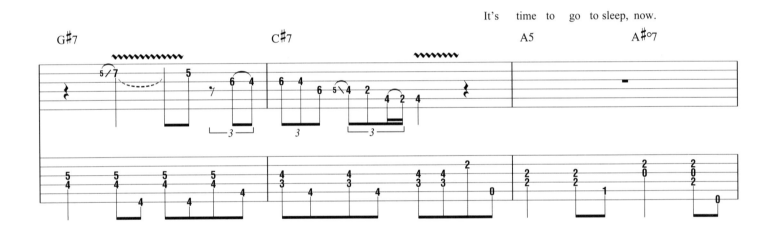

Free time

*   *rit.*

Lit - tle man, you've had   a   bus - y   day.

E   C#m7   F#m7   B7   Fmaj9/A   E

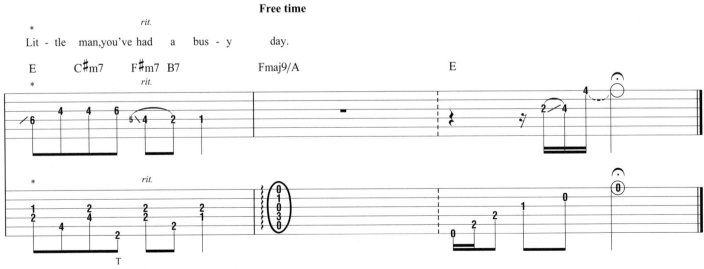

*Played/sung as straight eighth-notes.

Stones in My Passway

Words and Music by Robert Johnson

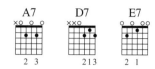

Gtr. 1: Open A tuning:
(low to high) E-A-E-A-C♯-E

Key of A
Intro
Moderately slow ♩ = 90

1. I got

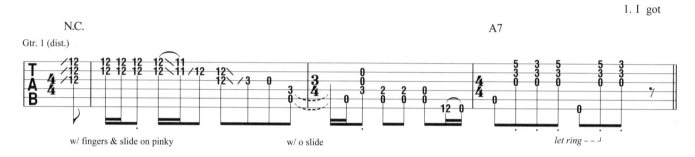

w/ fingers & slide on pinky   w/ o slide   let ring

Verse

stones   in my pass-way,   and my road   seem dark   as night.

I got stones   in my pass-way,   and my road seem dark as night.

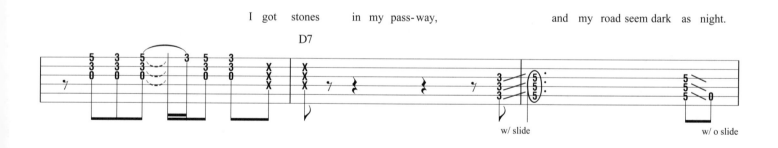

w/ slide   w/ o slide

I got   pain in my heart

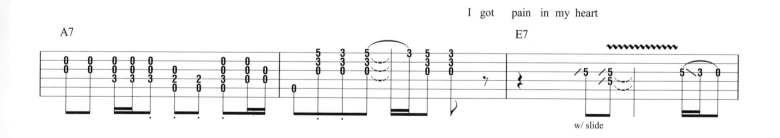

w/ slide

that have tak-en my ap - pe - tite.

2. I have a

D7   A7

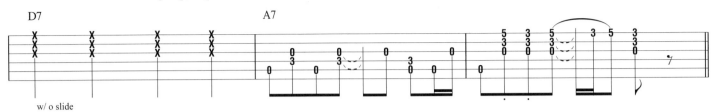

w/ o slide

Verse

bird   to whis - tle,   and I have a bird to sing.

A7

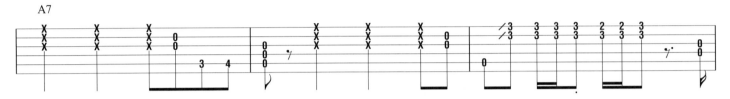

I have a bird   to whis - tle   and I have a bird to sing.

D7

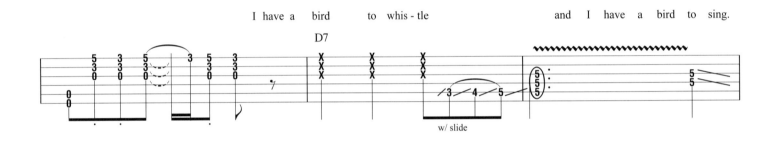

w/ slide

I get a wom-an that I'm lov - in',

A7   E7

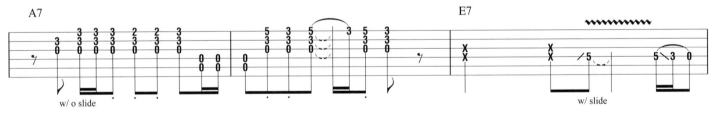

w/ o slide   w/ slide

boy, but she don't mean a thing.   3. My en - e-mies

D7   A7

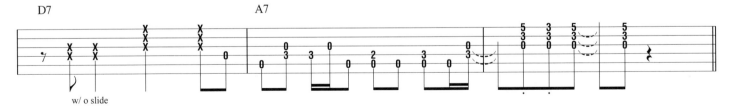

w/ o slide

46

Verse

have   be - trayed   me,   have   o - ver-tak - en   poor   Bob - by's   life.

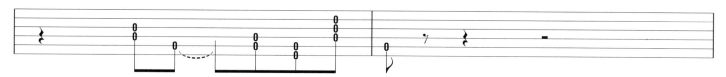

Ene - e-mies   have be - trayed   me,

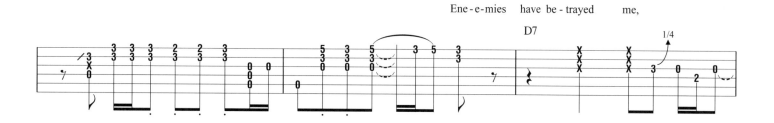

have   o - ver - tak - en poor   Bob-by's life.   And there's

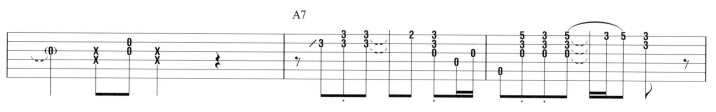

one   thing   cer - tain - ly,   they   have   stones   all   in   my path.

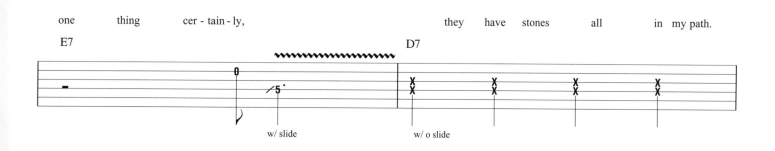

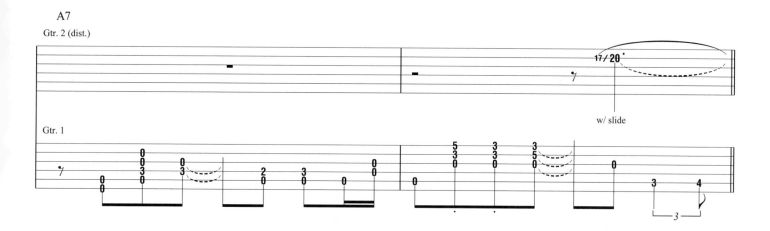

Verse

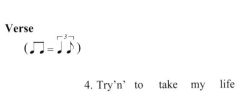

Gtr. 2 tacet

4. Try'n' to take my life   and   all   my   lov - in',   too.

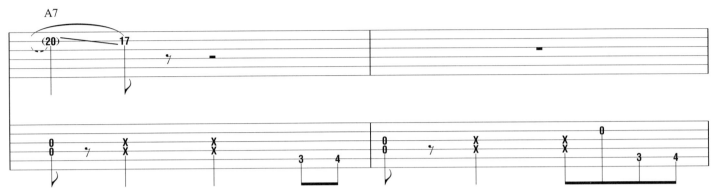

You   laid   a   path - way   for   me,   now,   what   are   you   try'n'   to   do?   And   I'm   cry'n'   please,

please   let   us   be   friends.

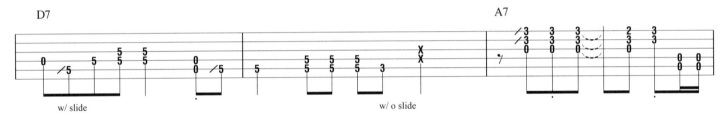

Hear   me,   hear   me   howl - in'   in   my   path - way,   rid - er.

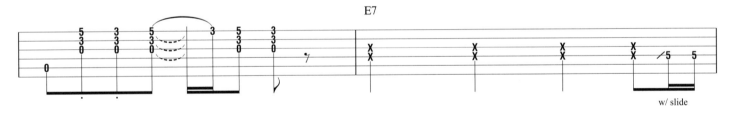

Please,   don't you, don't let me in.

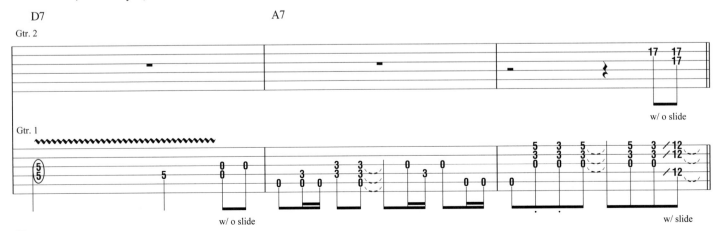

Guitar Solo

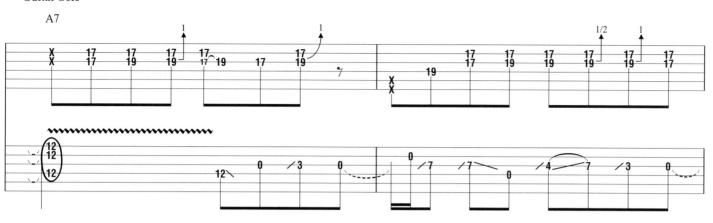

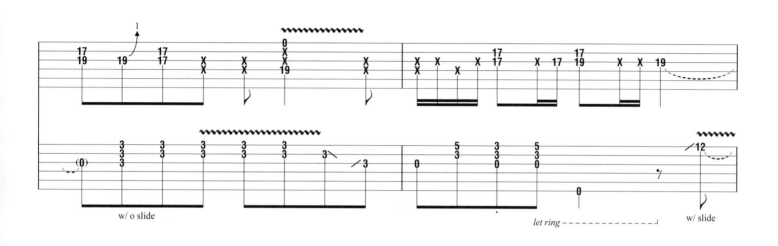

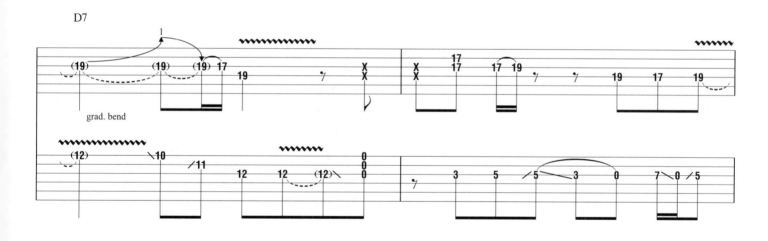

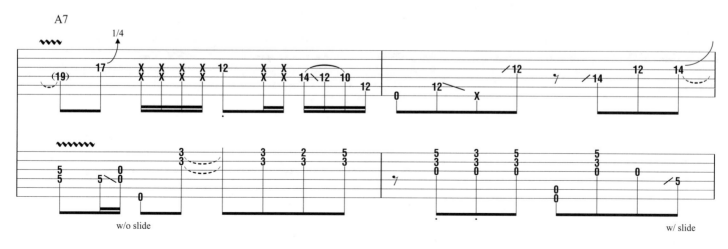

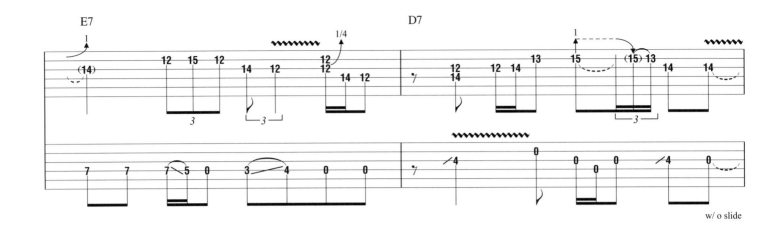

5. I got

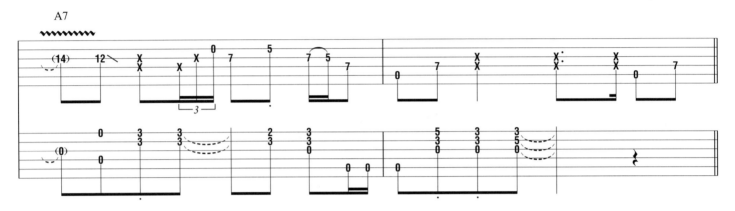

Verse

Gtr. 2 tacet

three   legs   to   truck   on.   Boys,   please   don't   block   my   road.

A7

Gtr. 1

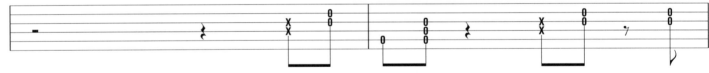

I   got

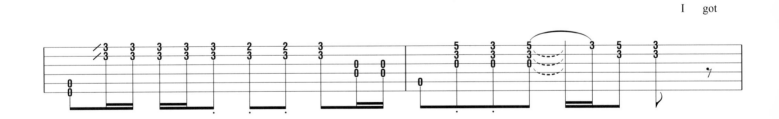

three   legs   to   truck   on.   Boys,   please   don't   block   my

D7

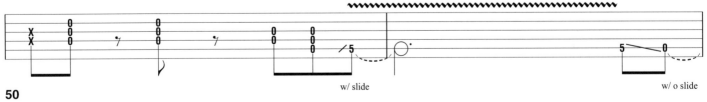

road.   Feel - in' a -

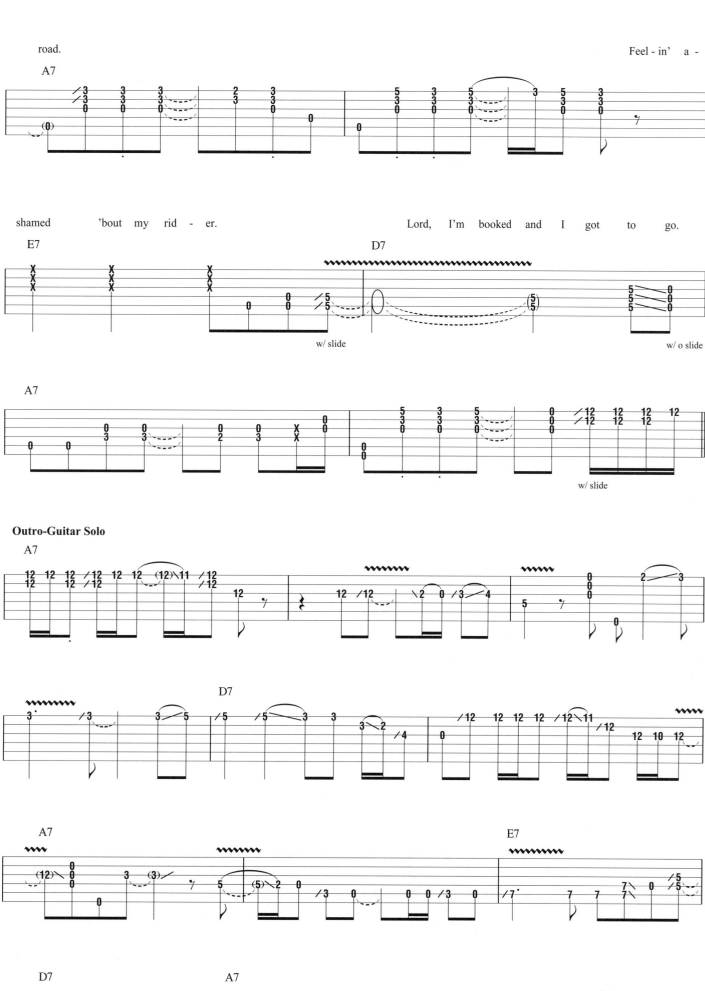

shamed   'bout my rid - er.   Lord, I'm booked and I got to go.

Outro-Guitar Solo

I Dreamed I Saw St. Augustine

By Bob Dylan

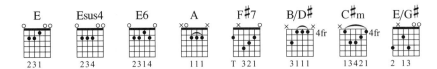

Key of E
Intro
Slow ♩ = 66

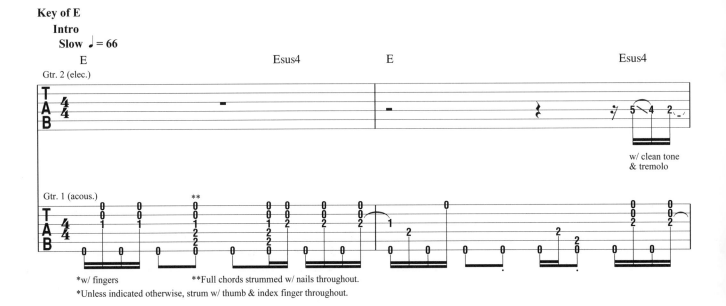

*w/ fingers   **Full chords strummed w/ nails throughout.
*Unless indicated otherwise, strum w/ thumb & index finger throughout.

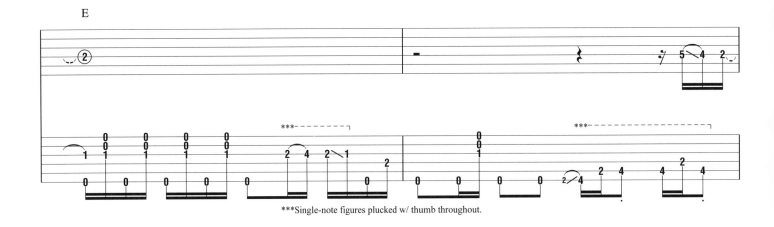

***Single-note figures plucked w/ thumb throughout.

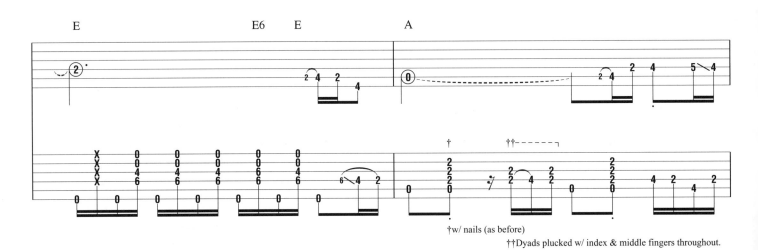

†w/ nails (as before)

††Dyads plucked w/ index & middle fingers throughout.

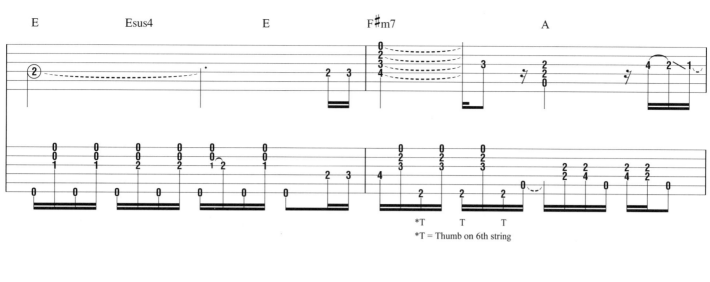

E   Esus4   E   F♯m7   A

*T = Thumb on 6th string

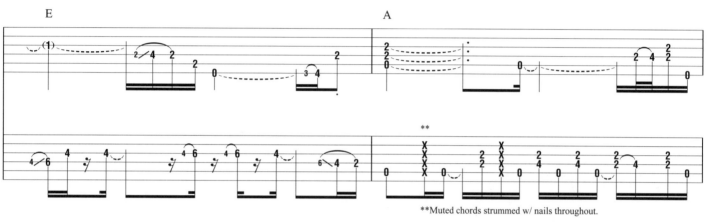

E   A

**Muted chords strummed w/ nails throughout.

1. I dreamed

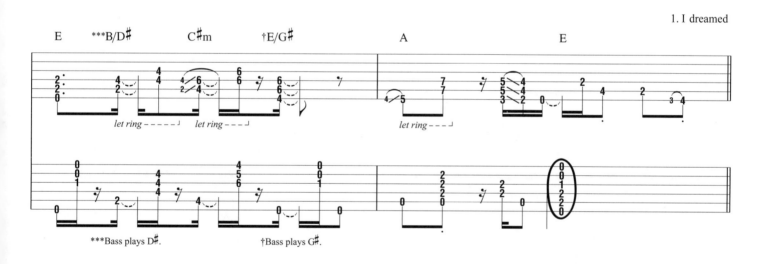

E ***B/D♯ C♯m †E/G♯   A   E

let ring let ring   let ring

***Bass plays D♯.   †Bass plays G♯.

Verse

I saw St. Au - gus - tine a - live as you or me,

E   A

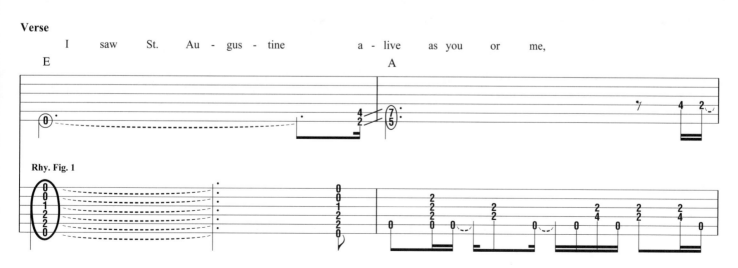

Rhy. Fig. 1

tear-ing   through   these   quar - ters   in   the   ut-most   mis - er - y.   With a blan-

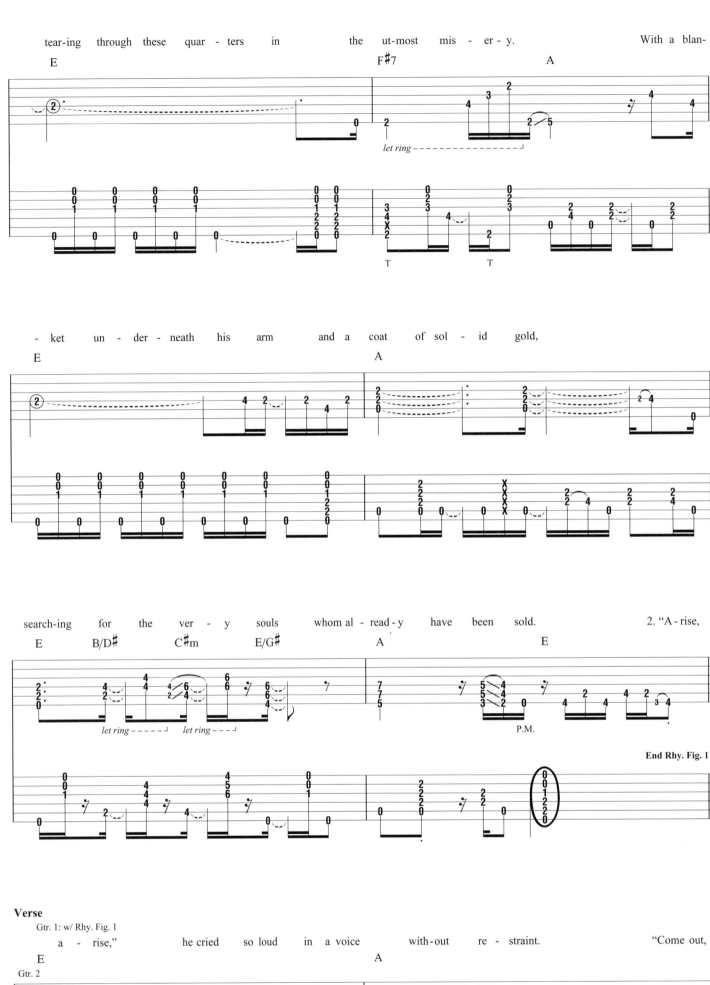

- ket   un - der - neath   his   arm   and   a   coat   of   sol - id   gold,

search-ing   for   the   ver - y   souls   whom al - read - y   have   been   sold.   2. "A - rise,

Verse

Gtr. 1: w/ Rhy. Fig. 1

a - rise,"   he cried   so loud   in   a voice   with-out   re - straint.   "Come out,

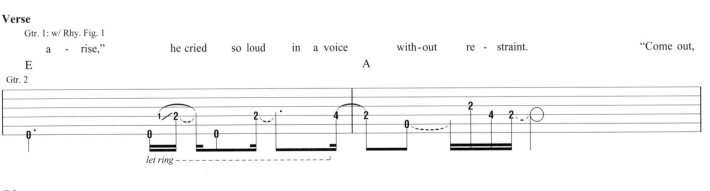

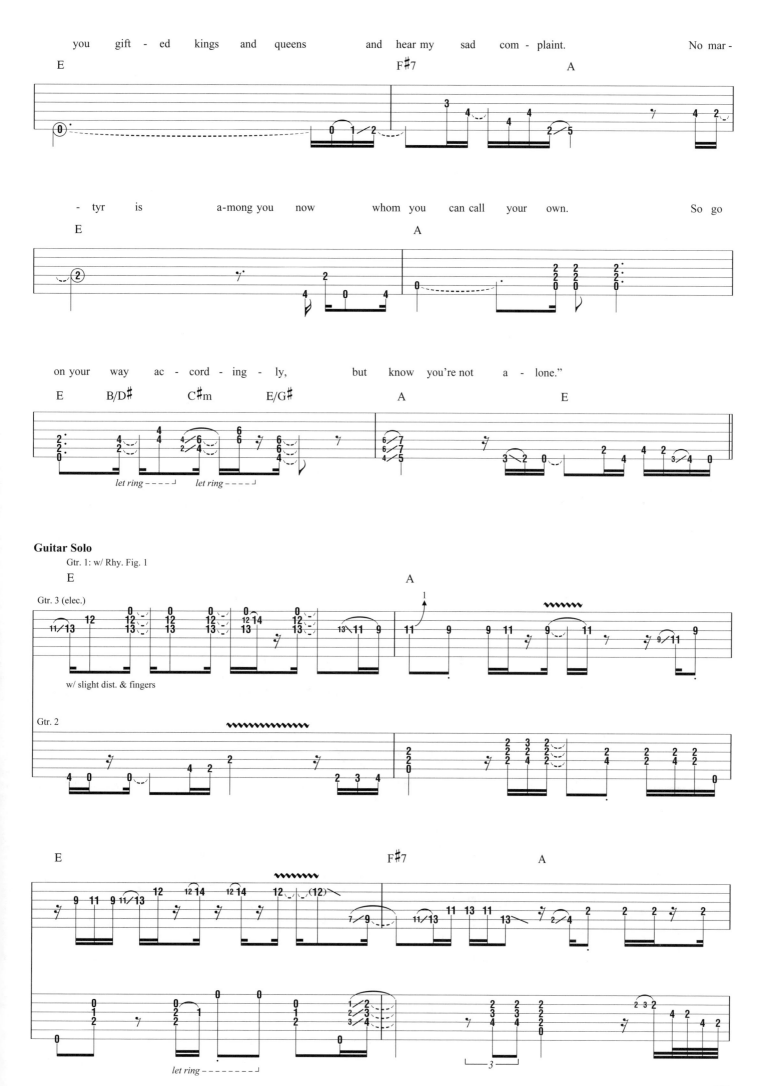

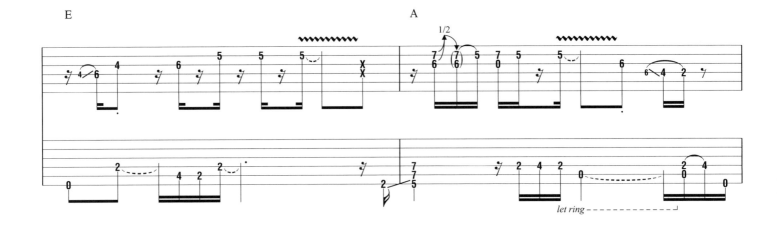

3. I dreamed

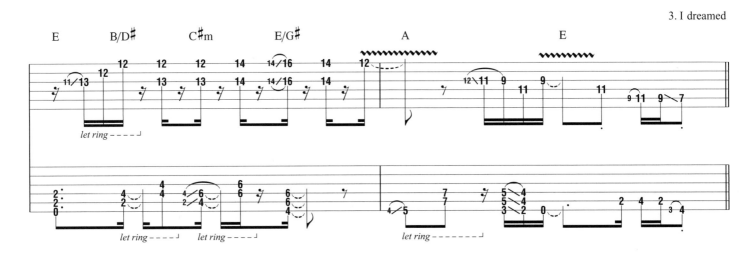

Verse
Gtr. 1: w/ Rhy. Fig. 1

I saw St. Aug - us - tine   a - live with fi - er - y   breath.   I dreamed

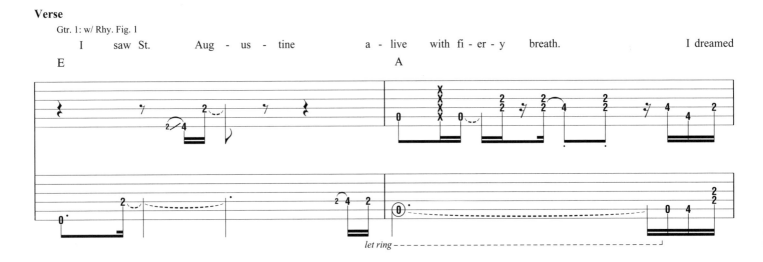

I was a - mong the ones   that put him out to death.   Oh, I

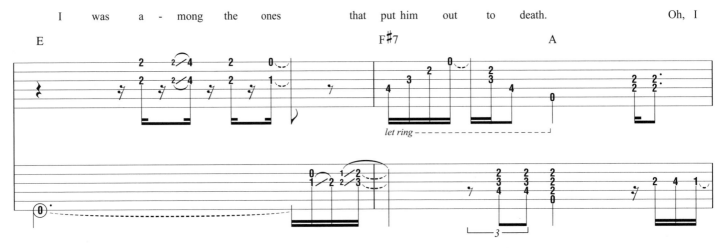

a - woke in an - ger, so a - lone and ter - ri - fied. I

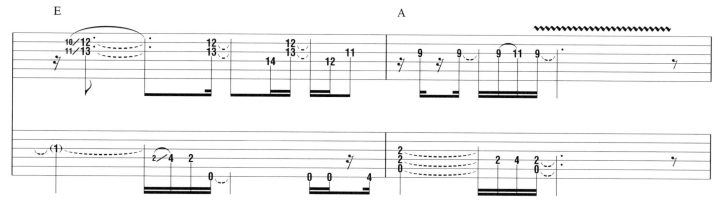

put my fin - gers a-gainst the glass and bowed my head and cried.

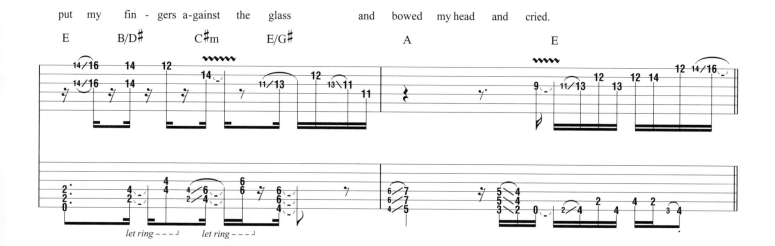

Outro-Guitar Solo

Gtr. 1: w/ Rhy. Fig. 1 (1 3/4 times)

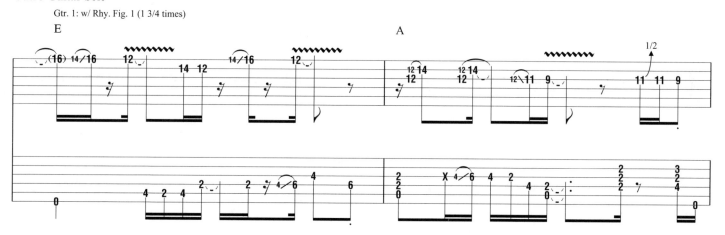

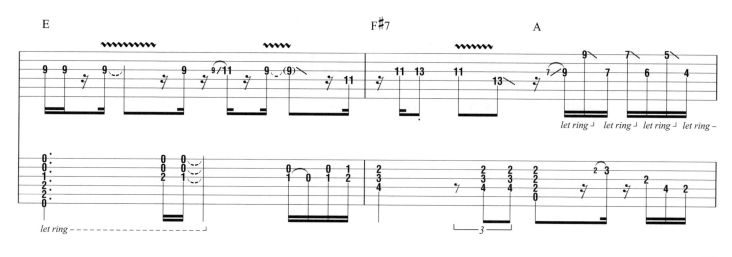

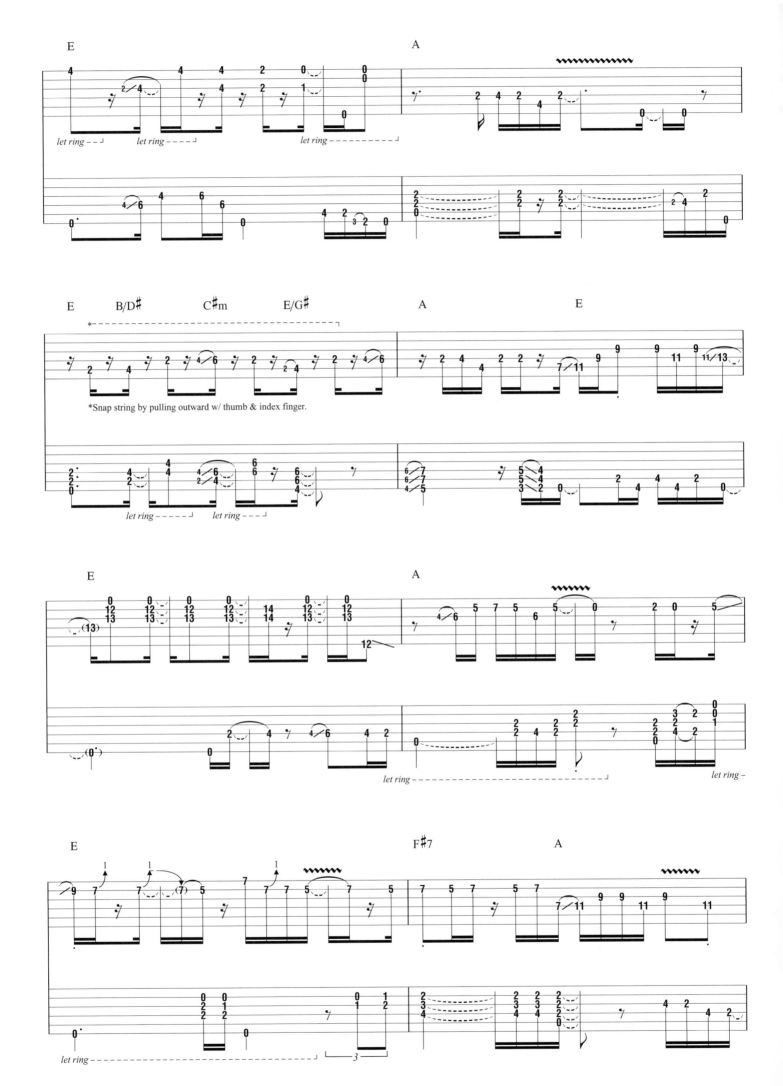

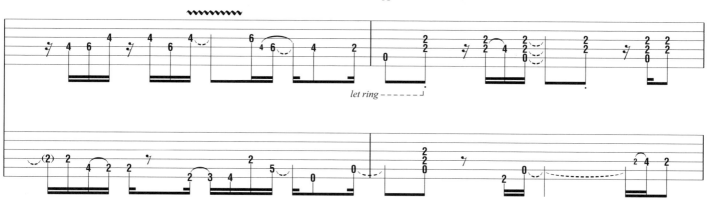

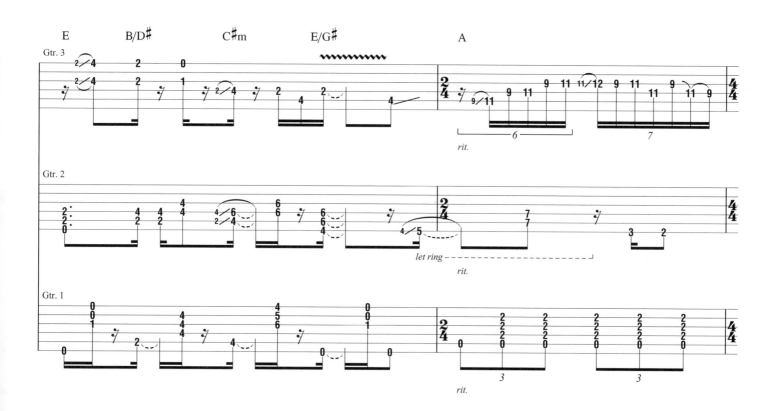

Free time

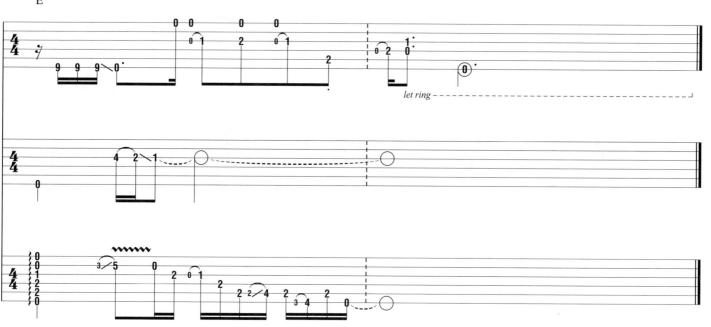

I'll Be Alright

Traditional

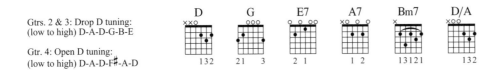

Gtrs. 2 & 3: Drop D tuning:
(low to high) D-A-D-G-B-E

Gtr. 4: Open D tuning:
(low to high) D-A-D-F♯-A-D

Key of D

Intro

Slow ♩ = 74

Half-time feel

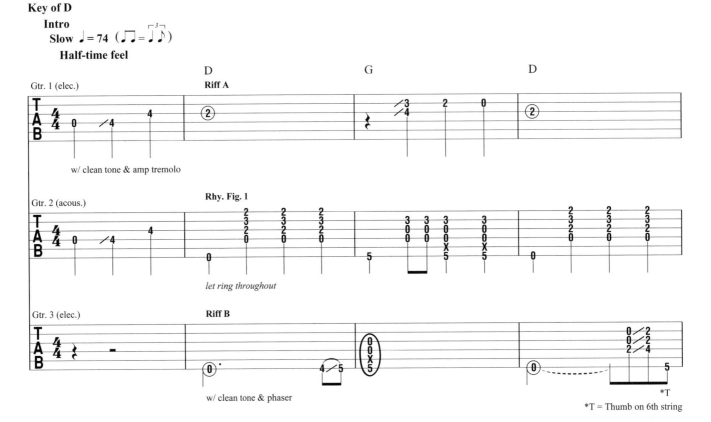

w/ clean tone & amp tremolo

Rhy. Fig. 1

let ring throughout

Riff B

w/ clean tone & phaser

*T = Thumb on 6th string

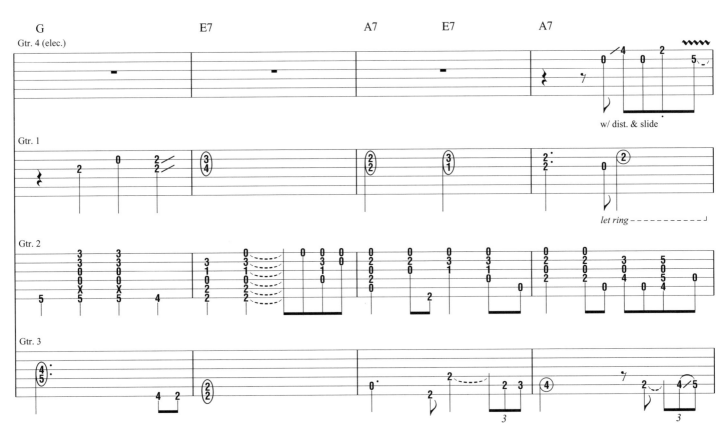

w/ dist. & slide

let ring

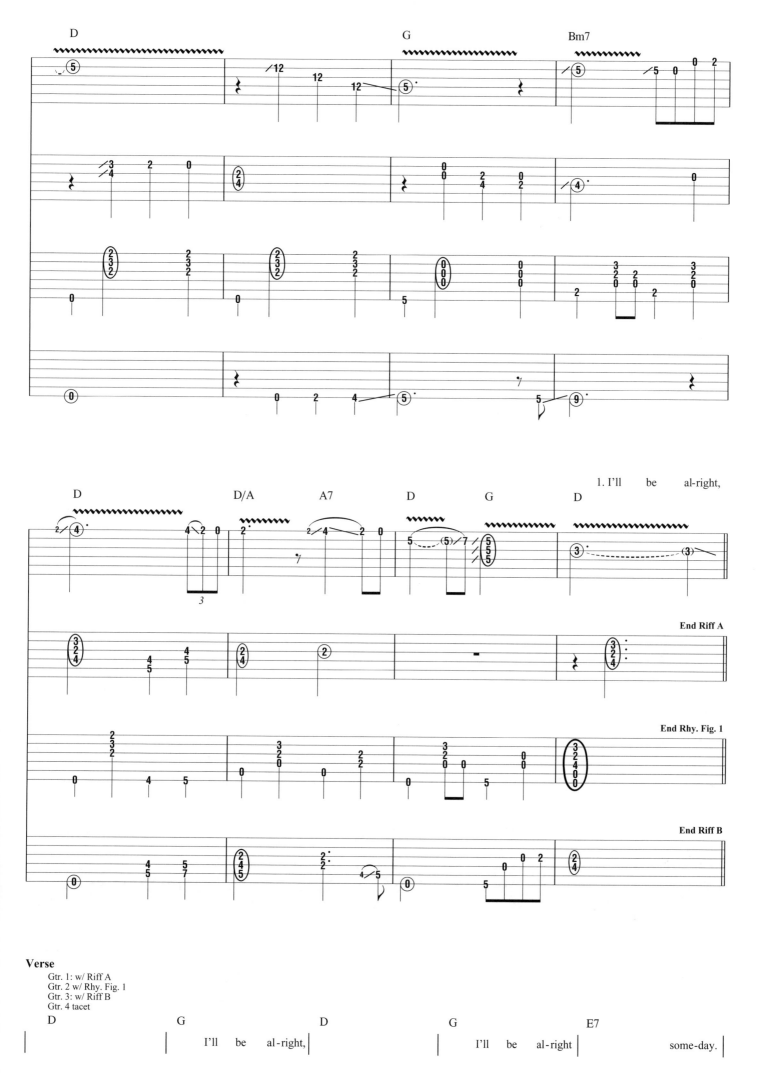

Verse

Gtr. 1: w/ Riff A
Gtr. 2 w/ Rhy. Fig. 1
Gtr. 3: w/ Riff B
Gtr. 4 tacet

D	G	D	G	E7
	I'll be al-right,		I'll be al-right	some-day.

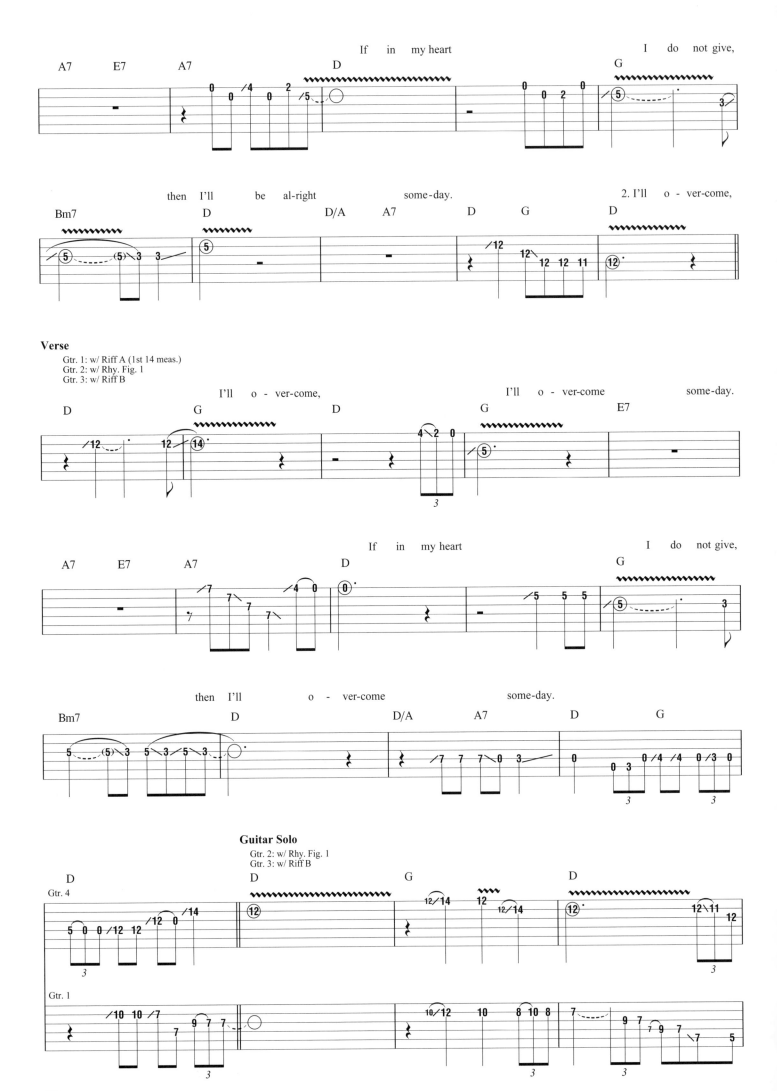

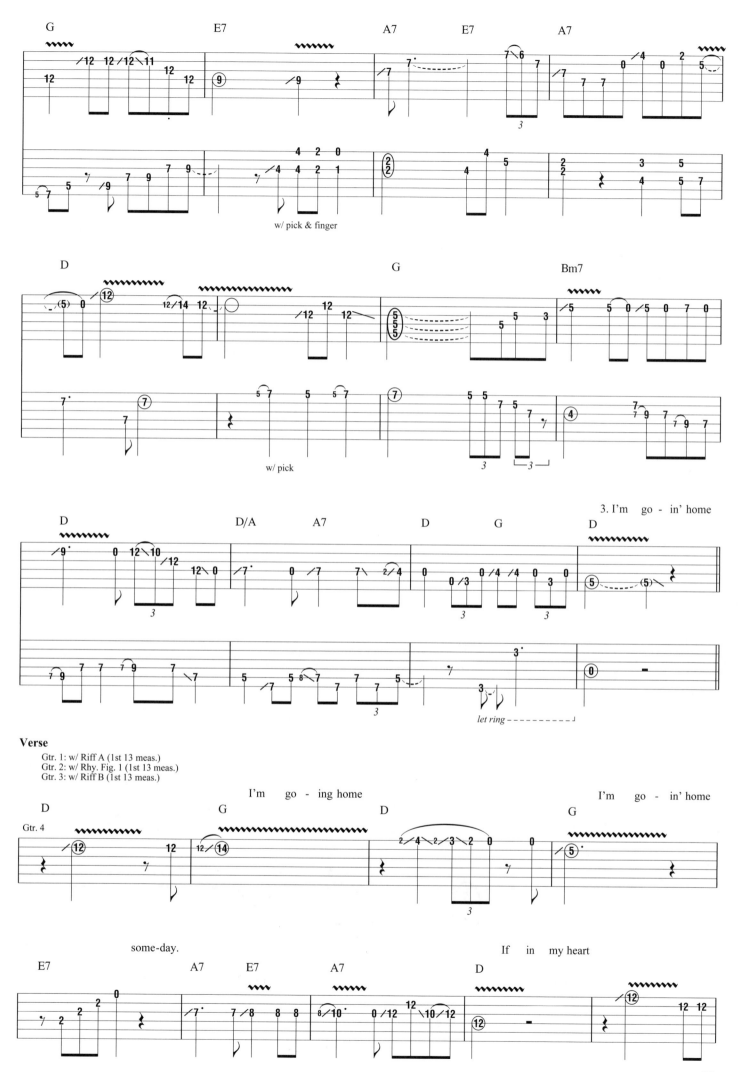

Somebody's Knockin'

Words and Music by J.J. Cale

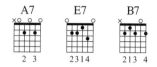

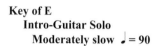

Key of E
Intro-Guitar Solo
Moderately slow ♩ = 90

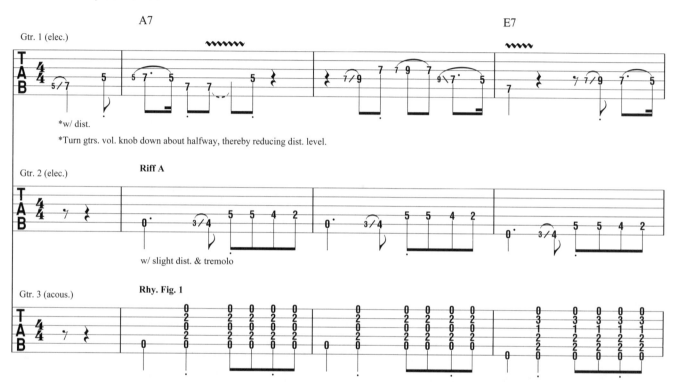

*w/ dist.

*Turn gtrs. vol. knob down about halfway, thereby reducing dist. level.

w/ slight dist. & tremolo

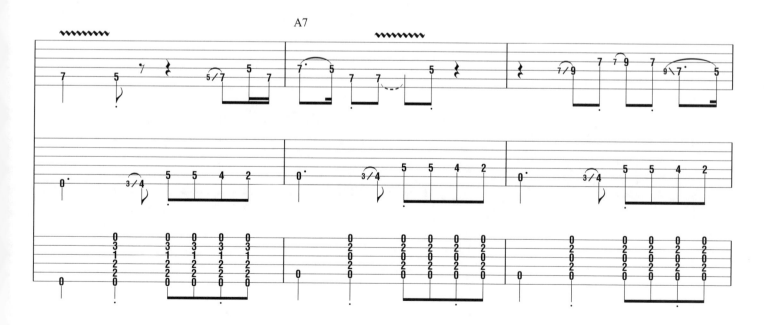

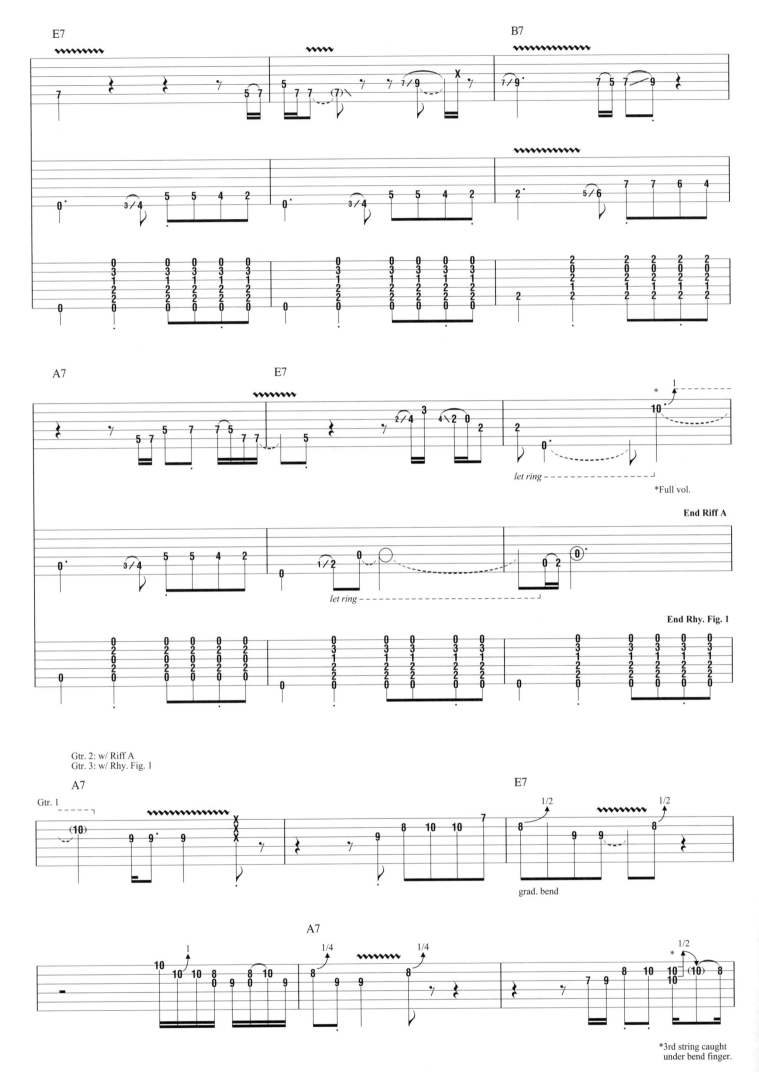

E7

A7   E7

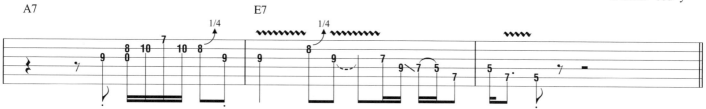

1. Some - bod - y

Verse

Gtr. 2: w/ Riff A
Gtr. 3: w/ Rhy. Fig. 1

knock - in',   some - bod - y knock - in' at my door.

A7   E7

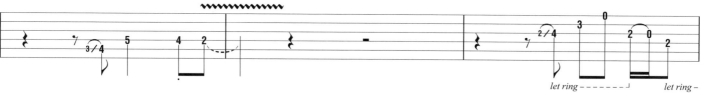

Some - bod - y knock - in',   some - bod - y knock - in' on my

           A7

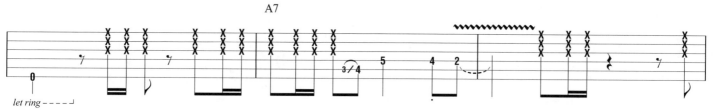

door.   Well, it must be   my wom - an

E7   B7

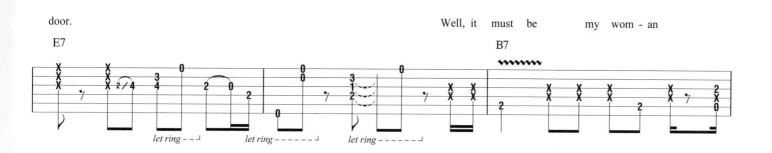

com - in' 'round here   for   more.   2. Some-bod - y

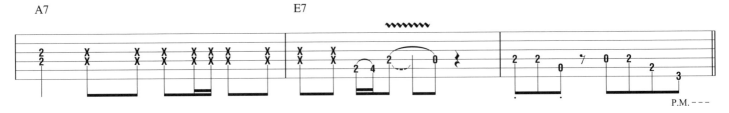

Verse

Gtr. 2: w/ Riff A
Gtr. 3: w/ Rhy. Fig. 1

whis - pered,   some - bod - y whis - pered in   my   ear.

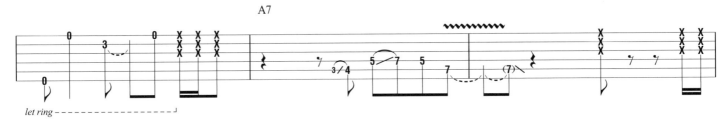

Some - bod - y   whis - pered,   some - bod - y whis - pered in my

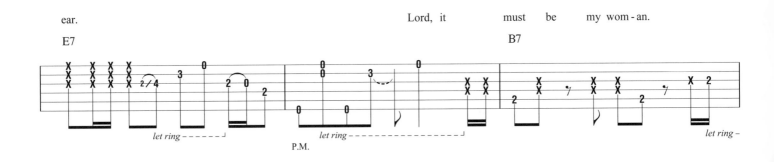

ear.   Lord, it   must   be   my wom - an.

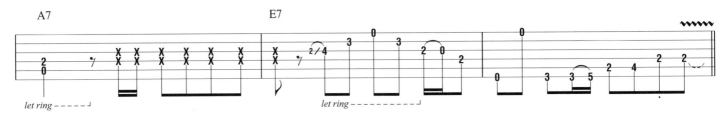

I can feel her when she's   near.

Piano/Organ Solo

Gtr. 2: w/ Riff A (2 times)
Gtr. 3: w/ Rhy. Fig. 1 (2 times)
2nd time, Gtr. 1: w/ Rhy. Fill 1

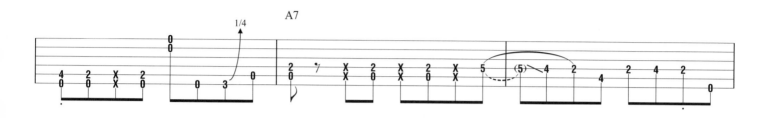

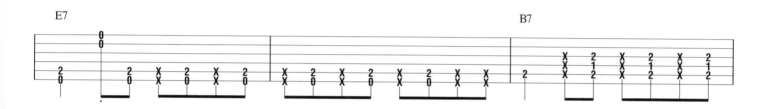

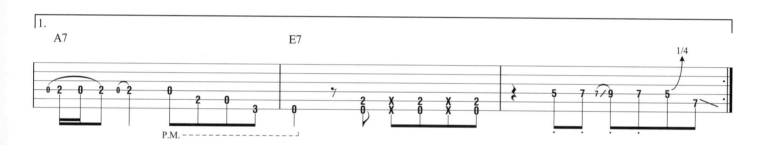

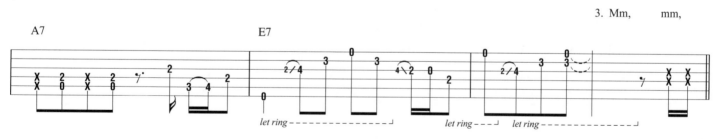

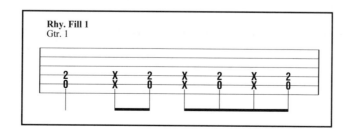

Verse

Gtr. 2: w/ Riff A
Gtr. 3: w/ Rhy. Fig. 1

mm,   mm, mm,   she can get right   down.   (Right   down.)

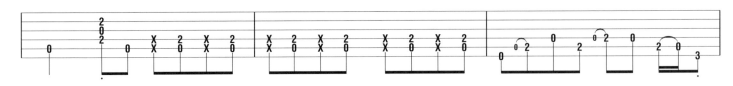

Mm,   mm,   mm,   mm, mm,   she can get right   down.

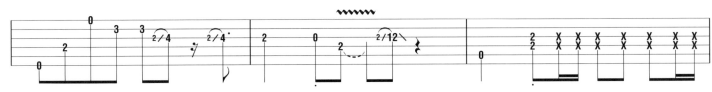

(Right   down.)   Lord,   it   must   be   my wom-an,

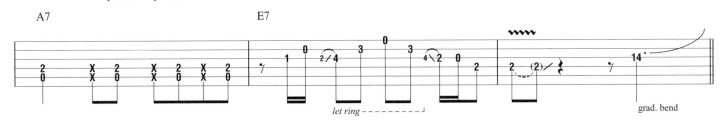

pick me up when I   am   down.

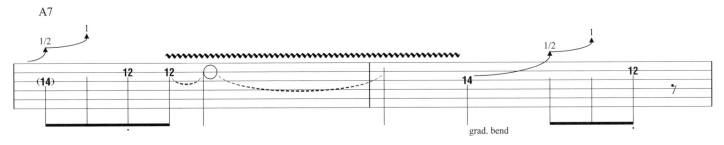

Guitar Solo

Gtr. 2: w/ Riff A (1st 10 meas.)
Gtr. 3: w/ Rhy. Fig. 1

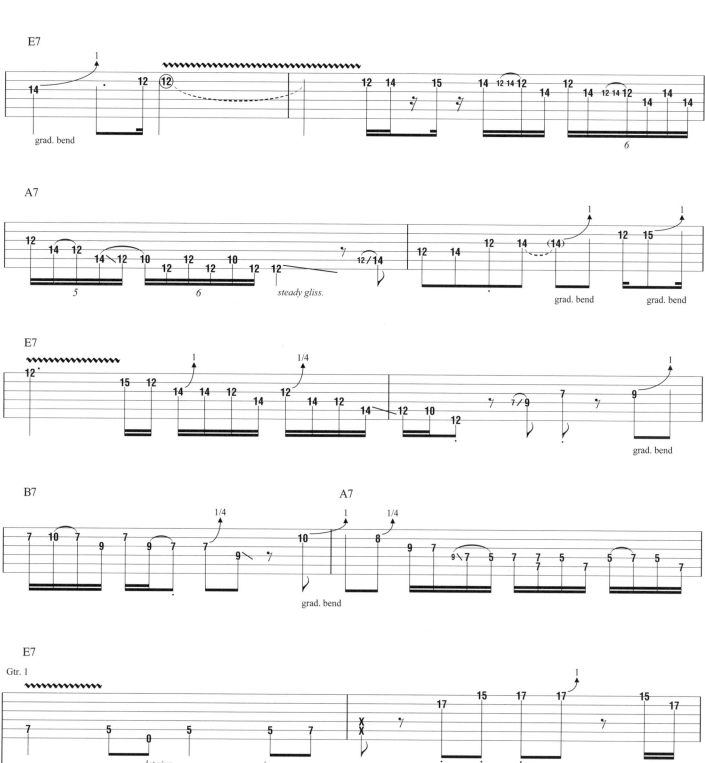

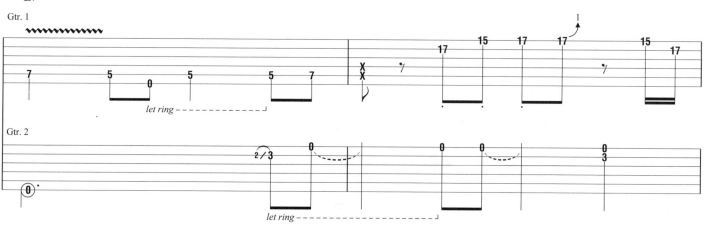

Gtr. 2: w/ Riff A (1st 10 meas.)
Gtr. 3: w/ Rhy. Fig. 1 (1st 10 meas.)

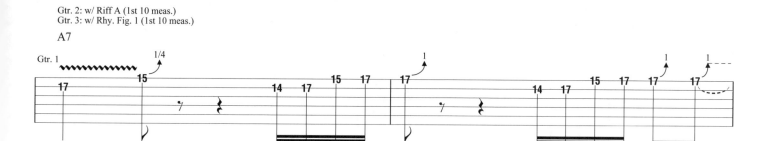

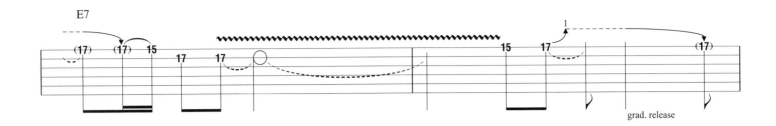

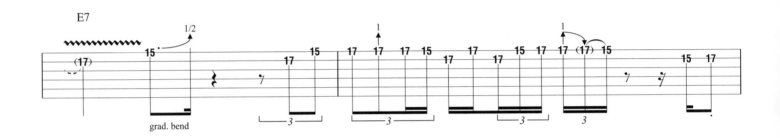

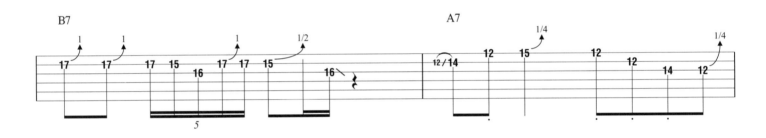

Free time

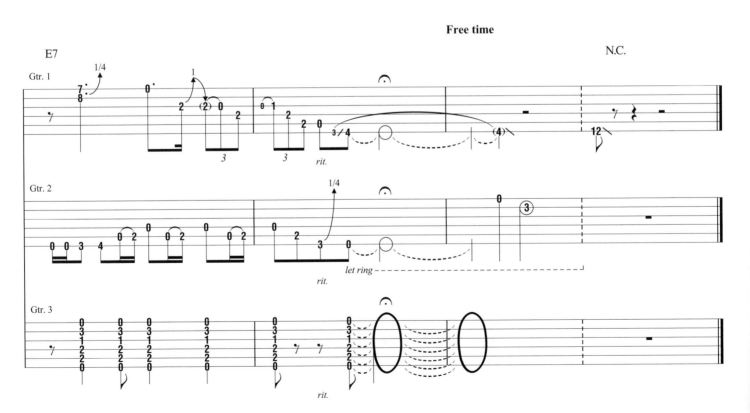

I'll Be Seeing You

Written by Irving Kahal and Sammy Fain

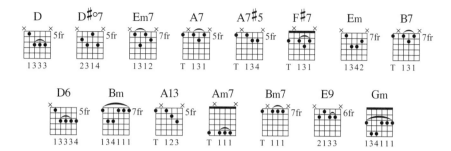

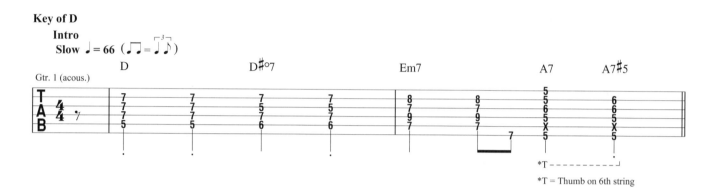

*T = Thumb on 6th string

Verse

1. And I'll be see-ing you in all the old fa-mil-iar plac-es

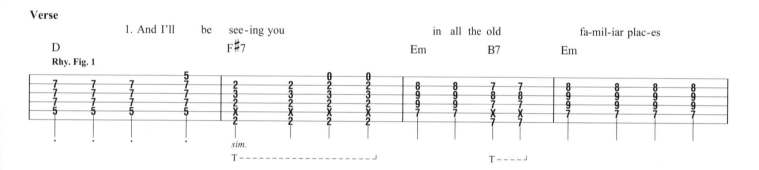

that this heart of mine em-brac-es all day through.

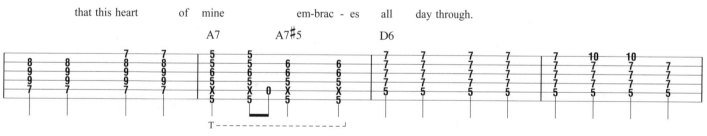

In that small ca-fé, the park a-cross the way,

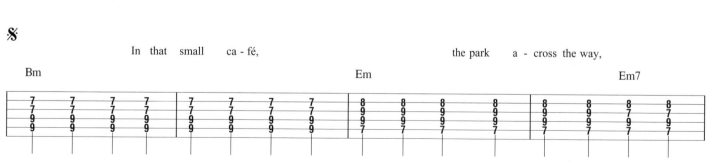

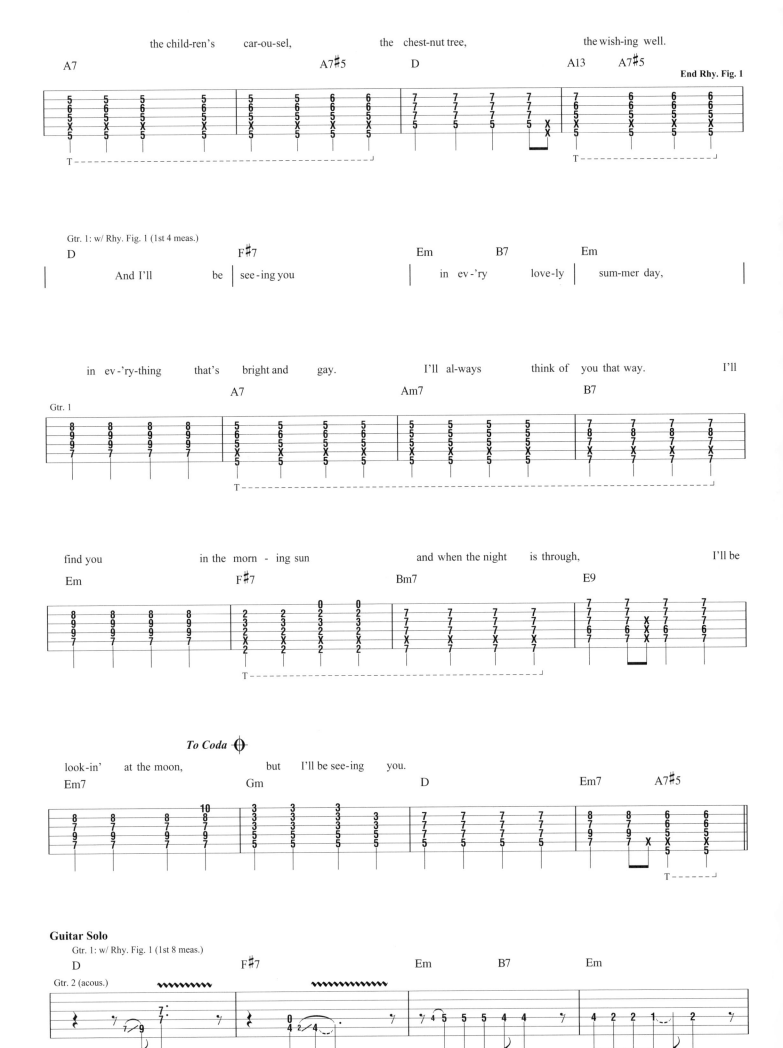

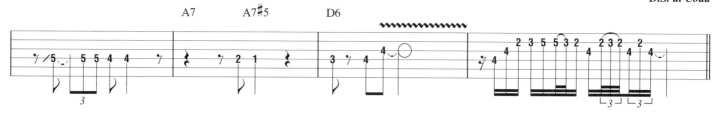

⊕ Coda

Outro-Guitar Solo

Gtr. 1: w/ Rhy. Fig. 1 (till fade)

but I'll be see - ing you.

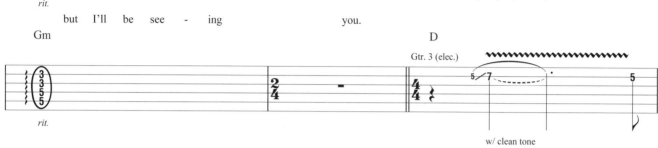

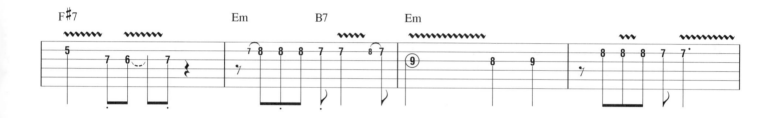

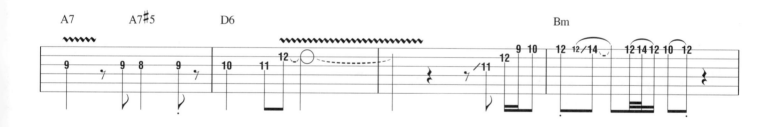

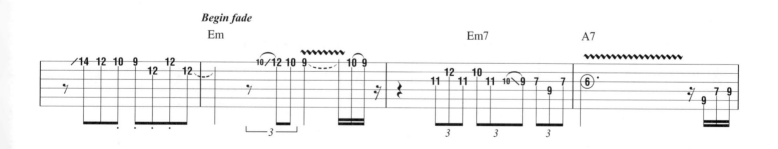

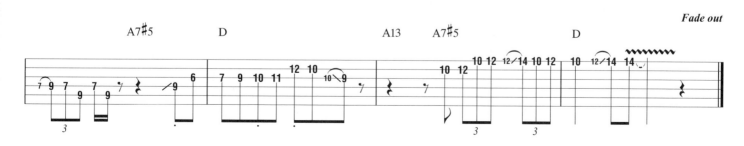

RHYTHM TAB LEGEND

Rhythm Tab is a form of notation that adds rhythmic values to the traditional tab staff.

TABLATURE graphically represents the guitar fingerboard. Each horizontal line represents a string, and each number represents a fret. Rhythmic values are shown using ovals, stems, and dots.

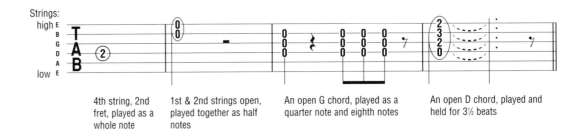

4th string, 2nd fret, played as a whole note

1st & 2nd strings open, played together as half notes

An open G chord, played as a quarter note and eighth notes

An open D chord, played and held for 3½ beats

Definitions for Special Guitar Notation

HALF-STEP BEND: Strike the note and bend up 1/2 step.

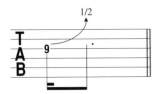

WHOLE-STEP BEND: Strike the note and bend up one step.

GRACE NOTE BEND: Strike the note and immediately bend up as indicated.

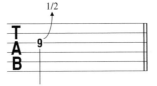

SLIGHT (MICROTONE) BEND: Strike the note and bend up 1/4 step.

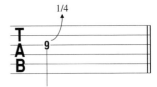

BEND AND RELEASE: Strike the note and bend up as indicated, then release back to the original note. Only the first note is struck.

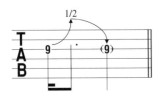

PRE-BEND: Bend the note as indicated, then strike it.

PRE-BEND AND RELEASE: Bend the note as indicated. Strike it and release the bend back to the original note.

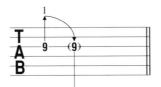

UNISON BEND: Strike the two notes simultaneously and bend the lower note up to the pitch of the higher.

HOLD BEND: While sustaining bent note, strike note on different string.

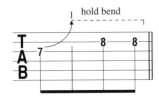

VIBRATO: The string is vibrated by rapidly bending and releasing the note with the fretting hand.

WIDE VIBRATO: The pitch is varied to a greater degree by vibrating with the fretting hand.

HAMMER-ON: Strike the first (lower) note with one finger, then sound the higher note (on the same string) with another finger by fretting it without picking.

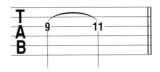

PULL-OFF: Place both fingers on the notes to be sounded. Strike the first note and without picking, pull the finger off to sound the second (lower) note.

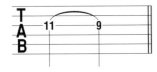

HAMMER FROM NOWHERE: Sound note(s) by hammering with fret hand finger only.

GRACE NOTE SLUR: Strike the note and immediately hammer-on (or pull-off) as indicated.

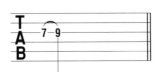

GRACE NOTE SLUR (CLUSTER): Strike the notes and immediately hammer-on (or pull-off) as indicated.

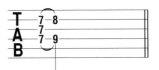

LEGATO SLIDE: Strike the first note and then slide the same fret-hand finger up or down to the second note. The second note is not struck.

SHIFT SLIDE: Same as legato slide, except the second note is struck.

TRILL: Very rapidly alternate between the notes indicated by continuously hammering on and pulling off.

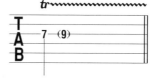

TAPPING: Hammer ("tap") the fret indicated with the pick-hand index or middle finger and pull off to the note fretted by the fret hand.

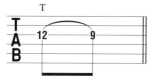

NATURAL HARMONIC: Strike the note while the fret-hand lightly touches the string directly over the fret indicated.

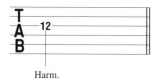

Harm.

PINCH HARMONIC: The note is fretted normally and a harmonic is produced by adding the edge of the thumb or the tip of the index finger of the pick hand to the normal pick attack.

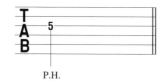

P.H.

HARP HARMONIC: The note is fretted normally and a harmonic is produced by gently resting the pick hand's index finger directly above the indicated fret (in parentheses) while the pick hand's thumb or pick assists by plucking the appropriate string.

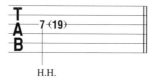

H.H.

PICK SCRAPE: The edge of the pick is rubbed down (or up) the string, producing a scratchy sound.

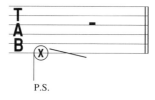

P.S.

MUFFLED STRINGS: A percussive sound is produced by laying the fret hand across the string(s) without depressing, and striking them with the pick hand.

PALM MUTING: The note is partially muted by the pick hand lightly touching the string(s) just before the bridge.

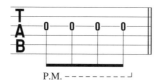

P.M. - - - - - - - - ⌐

RAKE: Drag the pick across the strings indicated with a single motion.

rake - - ⌐

TREMOLO PICKING: The note is picked as rapidly and continuously as possible.

ARPEGGIATE: Play the notes of the chord indicated by quickly rolling them from bottom to top.

VIBRATO BAR DIVE AND RETURN: The pitch of the note or chord is dropped a specified number of steps (in rhythm), then returned to the original pitch.

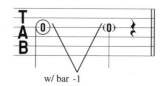

w/ bar -1

VIBRATO BAR SCOOP: Depress the bar just before striking the note, then quickly release the bar.

w/ bar - - - - - - - ⌐

VIBRATO BAR DIP: Strike the note and then immediately drop a specified number of steps, then release back to the original pitch.

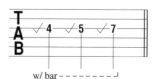

w/ bar - - - - - - ⌐

Additional Musical Definitions

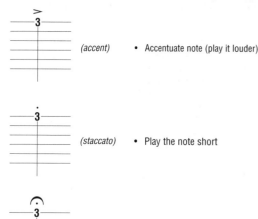

(accent) • Accentuate note (play it louder)

(staccato) • Play the note short

(fermata) • A hold or pause

• Downstroke

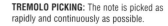

• Upstroke

• Repeat measures between signs

NOTE: Tablature numbers in parentheses are used when:
   • The note is sustained, but a new articulation begins (such as a hammer-on, pull-off, slide, or bend), or
   • A bend is released.

GUITAR RECORDED VERSIONS®

Guitar Recorded Versions® are note-for-note transcriptions of guitar music taken directly off recordings. This series, one of the most popular in print today, features some of the greatest guitar players and groups from blues and rock to country and jazz.

Guitar Recorded Versions are transcribed by the best transcribers in the business. Every book contains notes and tablature. Visit **www.halleonard.com** for our complete selection.

AUTHENTIC TRANSCRIPTIONS WITH NOTES AND TABLATURE

00690814	John 5 – Songs for Sanity	$19.95
00690751	John 5 – Vertigo	$19.95
00694912	Eric Johnson – Ah Via Musicom	$19.95
00690660	Best of Eric Johnson	$22.99
00691076	Eric Johnson – Up Close	$22.99
00690169	Eric Johnson – Venus Isle	$22.95
00122439	Jack Johnson – From Here to Now to You	$22.99
00690846	Jack Johnson and Friends – Sing-A-Longs and Lullabies for the Film Curious George	$19.95
00690271	Robert Johnson – The New Transcriptions	$24.99
00699131	Best of Janis Joplin	$19.95
00690427	Best of Judas Priest	$22.99
00690277	Best of Kansas	$19.95
00690911	Best of Phil Keaggy	$24.99
00690727	Toby Keith Guitar Collection	$19.99
00120814	Killswitch Engage – Disarm the Descent	$22.99
00690504	Very Best of Albert King	$19.95
00124869	Albert King with Stevie Ray Vaughan – In Session	$22.99
00130447	B.B. King – Live at the Regal	$17.99
00690444	B.B. King & Eric Clapton – Riding with the King	$22.99
00690134	Freddie King Collection	$19.95
00691062	Kings of Leon – Come Around Sundown	$22.99
00690157	Kiss – Alive!	$19.95
00690356	Kiss – Alive II	$22.99
00694903	Best of Kiss for Guitar	$24.95
00690355	Kiss – Destroyer	$16.95
14026320	Mark Knopfler – Get Lucky	$22.99
00690164	Mark Knopfler Guitar – Vol. 1	$19.95
00690163	Mark Knopfler/Chet Atkins – Neck and Neck	$19.95
00690780	Korn – Greatest Hits, Volume 1	$22.95
00690377	Kris Kristofferson Collection	$19.99
00690834	Lamb of God – Ashes of the Wake	$19.95
00690875	Lamb of God – Sacrament	$19.95
00690977	Ray LaMontagne – Gossip in the Grain	$19.99
00691057	Ray LaMontagne and the Pariah Dogs – God Willin' & The Creek Don't Rise	$22.99
00690922	Linkin Park – Minutes to Midnight	$19.95
00699623	The Best of Chuck Loeb	$19.95
00114563	The Lumineers	$22.99
00690525	Best of George Lynch	$24.99
00690955	Lynyrd Skynyrd – All-Time Greatest Hits	$22.99
00694954	New Best of Lynyrd Skynyrd	$19.95
00690577	Yngwie Malmsteen – Anthology	$24.95
00690754	Marilyn Manson – Lest We Forget	$19.95
00694956	Bob Marley – Legend	$19.95
00690548	Very Best of Bob Marley & The Wailers – One Love	$22.99
00694945	Bob Marley – Songs of Freedom	$24.95
00690914	Maroon 5 – It Won't Be Soon Before Long	$19.95
00690657	Maroon 5 – Songs About Jane	$19.95
00690748	Maroon 5 – 1.22.03 Acoustic	$19.95
00690989	Mastodon – Crack the Skye	$24.99
00119220	Brent Mason – Hot Wired	$19.99
00691176	Mastodon – The Hunter	$22.99
00137718	Mastodon – Once More 'Round the Sun	$22.99
00690616	Matchbox Twenty – More Than You Think You Are	$19.95
00691942	Andy McKee – Art of Motion	$22.99
00691034	Andy McKee – Joyland	$19.99
00120080	The Don McLean Songbook	$19.95
00694952	Megadeth – Countdown to Extinction	$22.95
00690244	Megadeth – Cryptic Writings	$19.95
00694951	Megadeth – Rust in Peace	$22.95
00690011	Megadeth – Youthanasia	$22.99
00690505	John Mellencamp Guitar Collection	$19.95
00690562	Pat Metheny – Bright Size Life	$19.95
00691073	Pat Metheny with Christian McBride & Antonion Sanchez – Day Trip/Tokyo Day Trip Live	$22.99
00690646	Pat Metheny – One Quiet Night	$19.95
00690559	Pat Metheny – Question & Answer	$19.95
00118836	Pat Metheny – Unity Band	$22.99
00102590	Pat Metheny – What's It All About	$22.99
00690040	Steve Miller Band Greatest Hits	$19.95
00119338	Ministry Guitar Tab Collection	$24.99
00102591	Wes Montgomery Guitar Anthology	$24.99
00694802	Gary Moore – Still Got the Blues	$22.99
00691005	Best of Motion City Soundtrack	$19.99
00129884	Jason Mraz – Yes!	$22.99
00690787	Mudvayne – L.D. 50	$22.95
00691070	Mumford & Sons – Sigh No More	$22.99
00118196	Muse – The 2nd Law	$19.99
00690996	My Morning Jacket Collection	$19.99
00690984	Matt Nathanson – Some Mad Hope	$22.99
00690611	Nirvana	$22.95
00694895	Nirvana – Bleach	$19.95
00694913	Nirvana – In Utero	$19.95
00694883	Nirvana – Nevermind	$19.95
00690026	Nirvana – Unplugged in New York	$19.95
00120112	No Doubt – Tragic Kingdom	$22.95
00690226	Oasis – The Other Side of Oasis	$19.95
00307163	Oasis – Time Flies... 1994-2009	$19.99
00690818	The Best of Opeth	$22.95
00691052	Roy Orbison – Black & White Night	$22.99
00694847	Best of Ozzy Osbourne	$22.95
00690399	Ozzy Osbourne – The Ozzman Cometh	$22.99
00690933	Best of Brad Paisley	$22.95
00690995	Brad Paisley – Play: The Guitar Album	$24.99
00690939	Christopher Parkening – Solo Pieces	$19.99
00690594	Best of Les Paul	$19.95
00694855	Pearl Jam – Ten	$22.99
00690439	A Perfect Circle – Mer De Noms	$19.95
00690725	Best of Carl Perkins	$19.99
00690499	Tom Petty – Definitive Guitar Collection	$19.99
00690868	Tom Petty – Highway Companion	$19.95
00690176	Phish – Billy Breathes	$22.95
00121933	Pink Floyd – Acoustic Guitar Collection	$22.99
00690428	Pink Floyd – Dark Side of the Moon	$19.95
00690789	Best of Poison	$19.95
00690299	Best of Elvis: The King of Rock 'n' Roll	$19.95
00692535	Elvis Presley	$19.95
00690925	The Very Best of Prince	$22.99
00690003	Classic Queen	$24.95
00694975	Queen – Greatest Hits	$24.95
00690670	Very Best of Queensryche	$19.95
00690878	The Raconteurs – Broken Boy Soldiers	$19.95
00109303	Radiohead Guitar Anthology	$24.99
00694910	Rage Against the Machine	$19.95
00119834	Rage Against the Machine – Guitar Anthology	$22.99
00690179	Rancid – And Out Come the Wolves	$22.95
00690426	Best of Ratt	$19.95
00690055	Red Hot Chili Peppers – Blood Sugar Sex Magik	$19.95
00690584	Red Hot Chili Peppers – By the Way	$19.95
00690379	Red Hot Chili Peppers – Californication	$19.95
00182634	Red Hot Chili Peppers – The Getaway	$24.99
00690673	Red Hot Chili Peppers – Greatest Hits	$19.95
00690090	Red Hot Chili Peppers – One Hot Minute	$22.95
00691166	Red Hot Chili Peppers – I'm with You	$22.99
00690852	Red Hot Chili Peppers – Stadium Arcadium	$24.95
00690511	Django Reinhardt – The Definitive Collection	$19.95
00690779	Relient K – MMHMM	$19.95
00690643	Relient K – Two Lefts Don't Make a Right ... But Three Do	$19.95
00690260	Jimmie Rodgers Guitar Collection	$19.95
14041901	Rodrigo Y Gabriela and C.U.B.A. – Area 52	$24.99
00690014	Rolling Stones – Exile on Main Street	$24.95
00690631	Rolling Stones – Guitar Anthology	$27.95
00690685	David Lee Roth – Eat 'Em and Smile	$19.95
00174797	Santana – IV*	$22.99
00690031	Santana's Greatest Hits	$19.95
00690796	Very Best of Michael Schenker	$19.95
00128870	Matt Schofield Guitar Tab Collection	$22.99
00690566	Best of Scorpions	$22.95
00690604	Bob Seger – Guitar Anthology	$22.99
00138870	Ed Sheeran – X	$19.99
00690803	Best of Kenny Wayne Shepherd Band	$19.95
00690750	Kenny Wayne Shepherd – The Place You're In	$19.95
00690857	Shinedown – Us and Them	$19.95
00122218	Skillet – Rise	$22.99
00691114	Slash – Guitar Anthology	$24.99
00690872	Slayer – Christ Illusion	$19.95
00690813	Slayer – Guitar Collection	$19.99
00690419	Slipknot	$19.95
00690973	Slipknot – All Hope Is Gone	$22.99
00690330	Social Distortion – Live at the Roxy	$19.95
00120004	Best of Steely Dan	$24.95
00694921	Best of Steppenwolf	$22.95
00690655	Best of Mike Stern	$19.95
14041588	Cat Stevens – Tea for the Tillerman	$19.99
00690949	Rod Stewart Guitar Anthology	$19.99
00690021	Sting – Fields of Gold	$19.95
00690520	Styx Guitar Collection	$19.95
00120081	Sublime	$19.99
00690992	Sublime – Robbin' the Hood	$19.99
00690519	SUM 41 – All Killer No Filler	$19.95
00691072	Best of Supertramp	$22.99
00690994	Taylor Swift	$22.99

RECORDED VERSIONS GUITAR®

AUTHENTIC TRANSCRIPTIONS WITH NOTES AND TABLATURE

00690993	Taylor Swift – Fearless	$22.99
00142151	Taylor Swift – 1989	$22.99
00115957	Taylor Swift – Red	$21.99
00691063	Taylor Swift – Speak Now	$22.99
00690767	Switchfoot – The Beautiful Letdown	$19.95
00690531	System of a Down – Toxicity	$19.95
00694824	Best of James Taylor	$19.99
00694887	Best of Thin Lizzy	$19.95
00690871	Three Days Grace – One-X	$19.95
00690891	30 Seconds to Mars – A Beautiful Lie	$19.95
00690233	The Merle Travis Collection	$19.99
00690683	Robin Trower – Bridge of Sighs	$19.95
00699191	U2 – Best of: 1980-1990	$19.95
00690732	U2 – Best of: 1990-2000	$19.95
00690894	U2 – 18 Singles	$19.95
00124461	Keith Urban – Guitar Anthology	$19.99
00690039	Steve Vai – Alien Love Secrets	$24.95
00690172	Steve Vai – Fire Garden	$24.95
00660137	Steve Vai – Passion & Warfare	$24.95
00690881	Steve Vai – Real Illusions: Reflections	$24.95
00694904	Steve Vai – Sex and Religion	$24.95
00110385	Steve Vai – The Story of Light	$22.99
00690392	Steve Vai – The Ultra Zone	$19.95
00700555	Van Halen – Van Halen	$19.99
00690024	Stevie Ray Vaughan – Couldn't Stand the Weather	$19.95
00690116	Stevie Ray Vaughan – Guitar Collection	$24.95
00660136	Stevie Ray Vaughan – In Step	$19.95
00694879	Stevie Ray Vaughan – In the Beginning	$19.95
00660058	Stevie Ray Vaughan – Lightnin' Blues '83-'87	$24.95
00694835	Stevie Ray Vaughan – The Sky Is Crying	$22.95
00690025	Stevie Ray Vaughan – Soul to Soul	$19.95
00690015	Stevie Ray Vaughan – Texas Flood	$19.99
00109770	Volbeat Guitar Collection	$22.99
00121808	Volbeat – Outlaw Gentlemen & Shady Ladies	$22.99
00183213	Volbeat – Seal the Deal & Let's Boogie*	$19.99
00690132	The T-Bone Walker Collection	$19.95
00150209	Trans-Siberian Orchestra Guitar Anthology	$19.99
00694789	Muddy Waters – Deep Blues	$24.95
00152161	Doc Watson – Guitar Anthology	$22.99
00690071	Weezer (The Blue Album)	$19.95
00690286	Weezer – Pinkerton	$19.95
00691046	Weezer – Rarities Edition	$22.99
00172118	Weezer (The White Album)*	$19.99
00117511	Whitesnake Guitar Collection	$19.99
00690447	Best of the Who	$24.95
00691941	The Who – Acoustic Guitar Collection	$22.99
00691006	Wilco Guitar Collection	$22.99
00690672	Best of Dar Williams	$19.95
00691017	Wolfmother – Cosmic Egg	$22.99
00690319	Stevie Wonder – Hits	$19.99
00690596	Best of the Yardbirds	$19.95
00690844	Yellowcard – Lights and Sounds	$19.95
00690916	The Best of Dwight Yoakam	$19.95
00691020	Neil Young – After the Goldrush	$22.99
00691019	Neil Young – Everybody Knows This Is Nowhere	$19.99
00690904	Neil Young – Harvest	$29.99
00691021	Neil Young – Harvest Moon	$22.99
00690905	Neil Young – Rust Never Sleeps	$19.99
00690443	Frank Zappa – Hot Rats	$19.95
00690624	Frank Zappa and the Mothers of Invention – One Size Fits All	$22.99
00690623	Frank Zappa – Over-Nite Sensation	$22.99
00121684	ZZ Top – Early Classics	$24.99
00690589	ZZ Top – Guitar Anthology	$24.95
00690960	ZZ Top Guitar Classics	$19.99

HAL•LEONARD®

*Tab transcriptions only.

Complete songlists and more at **www.halleonard.com**

Prices, contents, and availability subject to change without notice.

HAL•LEONARD
GUITAR PLAY-ALONG

AUDIO ACCESS INCLUDED

This series will help you play your favorite songs quickly and easily. Just follow the tab and listen to the audio to the hear how the guitar should sound, and then play along using the separate backing tracks. Audio files also include software to slow down the tempo without changing pitch. The melody and lyrics are included in the book so that you can sing or simply follow along.

INCLUDES TAB

VOL. 1 – ROCK	00699570 / $16.99
VOL. 2 – ACOUSTIC	00699569 / $16.99
VOL. 3 – HARD ROCK	00699573 / $17.99
VOL. 4 – POP/ROCK	00699571 / $16.99
VOL. 5 – MODERN ROCK	00699574 / $16.99
VOL. 6 – '90S ROCK	00699572 / $16.99
VOL. 7 – BLUES	00699575 / $16.95
VOL. 8 – ROCK	00699585 / $14.99
VOL. 9 – EASY ACOUSTIC SONGS	00151708 / $16.99
VOL. 10 – ACOUSTIC	00699586 / $16.95
VOL. 11 – EARLY ROCK	00699579 / $14.95
VOL. 12 – POP/ROCK	00699587 / $14.95
VOL. 13 – FOLK ROCK	00699581 / $15.99
VOL. 14 – BLUES ROCK	00699582 / $16.95
VOL. 15 – R&B	00699583 / $16.99
VOL. 16 – JAZZ	00699584 / $15.95
VOL. 17 – COUNTRY	00699588 / $15.95
VOL. 18 – ACOUSTIC ROCK	00699577 / $15.95
VOL. 19 – SOUL	00699578 / $14.99
VOL. 20 – ROCKABILLY	00699580 / $14.95
VOL. 22 – CHRISTMAS	00699600 / $15.95
VOL. 23 – SURF	00699635 / $15.99
VOL. 24 – ERIC CLAPTON	00699649 / $17.99
VOL. 25 – THE BEATLES	00198265 / $17.99
VOL. 26 – ELVIS PRESLEY	00699643 / $16.99
VOL. 27 – DAVID LEE ROTH	00699645 / $16.95
VOL. 28 – GREG KOCH	00699646 / $14.95
VOL. 29 – BOB SEGER	00699647 / $15.99
VOL. 30 – KISS	00699644 / $16.99
VOL. 31 – CHRISTMAS HITS	00699652 / $14.95
VOL. 32 – THE OFFSPRING	00699653 / $14.95
VOL. 33 – ACOUSTIC CLASSICS	00699656 / $16.95
VOL. 34 – CLASSIC ROCK	00699658 / $16.95
VOL. 35 – HAIR METAL	00699660 / $16.95
VOL. 36 – SOUTHERN ROCK	00699661 / $16.95
VOL. 37 – ACOUSTIC UNPLUGGED	00699662 / $22.99
VOL. 38 – BLUES	00699663 / $16.95
VOL. 39 – '80S METAL	00699664 / $16.99
VOL. 40 – INCUBUS	00699668 / $17.95
VOL. 41 – ERIC CLAPTON	00699669 / $16.95
VOL. 42 – 2000S ROCK	00699670 / $16.99
VOL. 43 – LYNYRD SKYNYRD	00699681 / $17.95
VOL. 44 – JAZZ	00699689 / $14.99
VOL. 45 – TV THEMES	00699718 / $14.95
VOL. 46 – MAINSTREAM ROCK	00699722 / $16.95
VOL. 47 – HENDRIX SMASH HITS	00699723 / $19.99
VOL. 48 – AEROSMITH CLASSICS	00699724 / $17.99
VOL. 49 – STEVIE RAY VAUGHAN	00699725 / $17.99
VOL. 50 – VAN HALEN 1978-1984	00110269 / $17.99
VOL. 51 – ALTERNATIVE '90S	00699727 / $14.99
VOL. 52 – FUNK	00699728 / $15.99
VOL. 53 – DISCO	00699729 / $14.99
VOL. 54 – HEAVY METAL	00699730 / $14.95
VOL. 55 – POP METAL	00699731 / $14.95
VOL. 56 – FOO FIGHTERS	00699749 / $15.99
VOL. 58 – BLINK-182	00699772 / $14.95
VOL. 59 – CHET ATKINS	00702347 / $16.99
VOL. 60 – 3 DOORS DOWN	00699774 / $14.95
VOL. 61 – SLIPKNOT	00699775 / $16.99
VOL. 62 – CHRISTMAS CAROLS	00699798 / $12.95
VOL. 63 – CREEDENCE CLEARWATER REVIVAL	00699802 / $16.99
VOL. 64 – THE ULTIMATE OZZY OSBOURNE	00699803 / $16.99

VOL. 66 – THE ROLLING STONES	00699807 / $16.95
VOL. 67 – BLACK SABBATH	00699808 / $16.99
VOL. 68 – PINK FLOYD – DARK SIDE OF THE MOON	00699809 / $16.99
VOL. 69 – ACOUSTIC FAVORITES	00699810 / $16.99
VOL. 70 – OZZY OSBOURNE	00699805 / $16.99
VOL. 71 – CHRISTIAN ROCK	00699824 / $14.95
VOL. 73 – BLUESY ROCK	00699829 / $16.99
VOL. 75 – TOM PETTY	00699882 / $16.99
VOL. 76 – COUNTRY HITS	00699884 / $14.95
VOL. 77 – BLUEGRASS	00699910 / $14.99
VOL. 78 – NIRVANA	00700132 / $16.99
VOL. 79 – NEIL YOUNG	00700133 / $24.99
VOL. 80 – ACOUSTIC ANTHOLOGY	00700175 / $19.95
VOL. 81 – ROCK ANTHOLOGY	00700176 / $22.99
VOL. 82 – EASY SONGS	00700177 / $14.99
VOL. 83 – THREE CHORD SONGS	00700178 / $16.99
VOL. 84 – STEELY DAN	00700200 / $16.99
VOL. 85 – THE POLICE	00700269 / $16.99
VOL. 86 – BOSTON	00700465 / $16.99
VOL. 87 – ACOUSTIC WOMEN	00700763 / $14.99
VOL. 88 – GRUNGE	00700467 / $16.99
VOL. 89 – REGGAE	00700468 / $15.99
VOL. 90 – CLASSICAL POP	00700469 / $14.99
VOL. 91 – BLUES INSTRUMENTALS	00700505 / $14.99
VOL. 92 – EARLY ROCK INSTRUMENTALS	00700506 / $14.99
VOL. 93 – ROCK INSTRUMENTALS	00700507 / $16.99
VOL. 94 – SLOW BLUES	00700508 / $16.99
VOL. 95 – BLUES CLASSICS	00700509 / $14.99
VOL. 96 – THIRD DAY	00700560 / $14.95
VOL. 97 – ROCK BAND	00700703 / $14.99
VOL. 99 – ZZ TOP	00700762 / $16.99
VOL. 100 – B.B. KING	00700466 / $16.99
VOL. 101 – SONGS FOR BEGINNERS	00701917 / $14.99
VOL. 102 – CLASSIC PUNK	00700769 / $14.99
VOL. 103 – SWITCHFOOT	00700773 / $16.99
VOL. 104 – DUANE ALLMAN	00700846 / $16.99
VOL. 105 – LATIN	00700939 / $16.99
VOL. 106 – WEEZER	00700958 / $14.99
VOL. 107 – CREAM	00701069 / $16.99
VOL. 108 – THE WHO	00701053 / $16.99
VOL. 109 – STEVE MILLER	00701054 / $16.99
VOL. 110 – SLIDE GUITAR HITS	00701055 / $16.99
VOL. 111 – JOHN MELLENCAMP	00701056 / $14.99
VOL. 112 – QUEEN	00701052 / $16.99
VOL. 113 – JIM CROCE	00701058 / $15.99
VOL. 114 – BON JOVI	00701060 / $14.99
VOL. 115 – JOHNNY CASH	00701070 / $16.99
VOL. 116 – THE VENTURES	00701124 / $14.99
VOL. 117 – BRAD PAISLEY	00701224 / $16.99
VOL. 118 – ERIC JOHNSON	00701353 / $16.99
VOL. 119 – AC/DC CLASSICS	00701356 / $17.99
VOL. 120 – PROGRESSIVE ROCK	00701457 / $14.99
VOL. 121 – U2	00701508 / $16.99
VOL. 122 – CROSBY, STILLS & NASH	00701610 / $16.99
VOL. 123 – LENNON & McCARTNEY ACOUSTIC	00701614 / $16.99
VOL. 125 – JEFF BECK	00701687 / $16.99
VOL. 126 – BOB MARLEY	00701701 / $16.99
VOL. 127 – 1970S ROCK	00701739 / $16.99
VOL. 128 – 1960S ROCK	00701740 / $14.99
VOL. 129 – MEGADETH	00701741 / $16.99
VOL. 130 – IRON MAIDEN	00701742 / $17.99
VOL. 131 – 1990S ROCK	00701743 / $14.99

VOL. 132 – COUNTRY ROCK	00701757 / $15.99
VOL. 133 – TAYLOR SWIFT	00701894 / $16.99
VOL. 134 – AVENGED SEVENFOLD	00701906 / $16.99
VOL. 136 – GUITAR THEMES	00701922 / $14.99
VOL. 137 – IRISH TUNES	00701966 / $15.99
VOL. 138 – BLUEGRASS CLASSICS	00701967 / $14.99
VOL. 139 – GARY MOORE	00702370 / $16.99
VOL. 140 – MORE STEVIE RAY VAUGHAN	00702396 / $17.99
VOL. 141 – ACOUSTIC HITS	00702401 / $16.99
VOL. 143 – SLASH	00702425 / $19.99
VOL. 144 – DJANGO REINHARDT	00702531 / $16.99
VOL. 145 – DEF LEPPARD	00702532 / $17.99
VOL. 146 – ROBERT JOHNSON	00702533 / $16.99
VOL. 147 – SIMON & GARFUNKEL	14041591 / $16.99
VOL. 148 – BOB DYLAN	14041592 / $16.99
VOL. 149 – AC/DC HITS	14041593 / $17.99
VOL. 150 – ZAKK WYLDE	02501717 / $16.99
VOL. 152 – JOE BONAMASSA	02501751 / $19.99
VOL. 153 – RED HOT CHILI PEPPERS	00702990 / $19.99
VOL. 155 – ERIC CLAPTON – FROM THE ALBUM UNPLUGGED	00703085 / $16.99
VOL. 156 – SLAYER	00703770 / $17.99
VOL. 157 – FLEETWOOD MAC	00101382 / $16.99
VOL. 158 – ULTIMATE CHRISTMAS	00101889 / $14.99
VOL. 159 – WES MONTGOMERY	00102593 / $19.99
VOL. 160 – T-BONE WALKER	00102641 / $16.99
VOL. 161 – THE EAGLES – ACOUSTIC	00102659 / $17.99
VOL. 162 – THE EAGLES HITS	00102667 / $17.99
VOL. 163 – PANTERA	00103036 / $17.99
VOL. 164 – VAN HALEN 1986-1995	00110270 / $17.99
VOL. 166 – MODERN BLUES	00700764 / $16.99
VOL. 167 – DREAM THEATER	00111938 / $24.99
VOL. 168 – KISS	00113421 / $16.99
VOL. 169 – TAYLOR SWIFT	00115982 / $16.99
VOL. 170 – THREE DAYS GRACE	00117337 / $16.99
VOL. 171 – JAMES BROWN	00117420 / $16.99
VOL. 172 – THE DOOBIE BROTHERS	00119670 / $16.99
VOL. 174 – SCORPIONS	00122119 / $16.99
VOL. 175 – MICHAEL SCHENKER	00122127 / $16.99
VOL. 176 – BLUES BREAKERS WITH JOHN MAYALL & ERIC CLAPTON	00122132 / $19.99
VOL. 177 – ALBERT KING	00123271 / $16.99
VOL. 178 – JASON MRAZ	00124165 / $17.99
VOL. 179 – RAMONES	00127073 / $16.99
VOL. 180 – BRUNO MARS	00129706 / $16.99
VOL. 181 – JACK JOHNSON	00129854 / $16.99
VOL. 182 – SOUNDGARDEN	00138161 / $17.99
VOL. 183 – BUDDY GUY	00138240 / $17.99
VOL. 184 – KENNY WAYNE SHEPHERD	00138258 / $17.99
VOL. 185 – JOE SATRIANI	00139457 / $17.99
VOL. 186 – GRATEFUL DEAD	00139459 / $17.99
VOL. 187 – JOHN DENVER	00140839 / $17.99
VOL. 188 – MÖTLEY CRUE	00141145 / $17.99
VOL. 189 – JOHN MAYER	00144350 / $17.99

Complete song lists available online.

Prices, contents, and availability subject to change without notice.

HAL•LEONARD®
www.halleonard.com

1016